The cc
focuses on st
I believe stu   ....
activities. Any time we can offer opportunities for students
to learn, grow, work, and succeed, we are doing them a
great service. Alexis Champneys Beckstead is admired in
our community for building a ballroom dance group from
scratch and giving us another reason to be proud of our
students. The positive impact that has been made in our
community and in the lives of the students involved has
been immeasurable. Our community is a better place and
these students are better people for having been involved
with Alexis and ballroom dancing.

~ **Joel Wilson, Superintendent**
Preston School District #201

This book captures the many possibilities that can
develop because of dancing and the influence it can have on
so many lives. Alexis Beckstead's love of ballroom dancing
shaped her life and the life of her family, but it has done
so much more. She has touched the lives of students. She
taught them how dancing can open doors of opportunities;
this is what each teacher should do. Through dance she has
taught them how to express themselves, how to work with
each other, and to expand their talents—the mark of a true
educator.

This book touched my heart. I had the chance to
know many of the students on her team, so I had a personal
connection. But the book touched me in many other ways. Her
students are sharing their talent, just as Alexis did. Ballroom
dance helped my former students become successful in their
education, their careers, and in their homes.

Thank you, Alexis, for writing this book and allowing
those of us who never learned how to dance to understand
the power of dancing.

~ **Barbara Taylor**
Former Preston High Principal and Superintendent

Printed in the United States of America
By Ecko House Publishing
P.O. Box 901930
Sandy, Utah 84092

Dance to Live -
How Ballroom Dance Gave Life to Me and My Community
A Memoir by Alexis Champneys Beckstead

ISBN-978-1-4276-5345-1

Dance to Live!

How Ballroom Dance Gave Life to Me and My Community

A Memoir by

Alexis Champneys Beckstead

Ecko House Publishing

To Susan Jensen, who taught me to dance as
a teenager and changed my life forever,

To Emerson Lyman for my
technical college training,

To my husband David who gave me a dancing
romance and supported my efforts to teach,

And also to my father, Floyd "Buzz" Champneys,
who taught me to enjoy living every day
and advised me to "dance to live!"

"And David danced before the Lord with all his might."
2 Samuel 6:14

"Let them praise his name in the dance."
Psalm 149:3

"Again I will build thee, and thou shalt be built, O virgin
of Israel: thou shalt again be adorned with thy tabrets, and
shalt go forth in the dances of them that make merry."
Jeremiah 31:4

Contents

PART III • The Influence of Dance

Preface

This is a true story and my purpose is to remind the world that a little ballroom dancing can have a big influence on our happiness. Remember your mother, father, or grandparents talking of dancing every weekend during those golden, big band days and how much fun it was? We can live it again. If this book encourages anyone to take a dance class, then it has been a success. If it inspires anyone knowledgeable in dancing to teach others, it has been a triumph.

The conversations in this story actually happened and have been recreated to the best of my ability. The people are all real. However, many of the names have been changed to avoid embarrassment or confusion of characters when names were repetitious.

I wish I could give an account of each student I taught, but it would never fit in this book. I was only able to focus on a minority. I am sorry if your tale was left out, but you are nonetheless dear to me and we both know what it meant to you to dance.

The reader might conclude that dancing was all I did. It was only a small part of my life. A fulfilling and happy existence is a well-rounded composition of many things. I advocate variety and moderation, with the spice of life being dance. Unfortunately, I have seen people go overboard on dancing to the point that it destroys relationships, drains pocketbooks, and limits the development of other elements. This can be avoided by keeping a proper perspective and using common sense. Conversely, the positive aspects of this art form are compelling and, if used with wisdom, can turn a boring life to one of brilliance.

I have focused on highlights to bring home the point that the arts—specifically the art of ballroom dancing—give us quality of life and build important character traits. This art just might save our young people, as it promotes mutual respect and friendship while teaching hard work and responsibility. The implementation of high school ballroom programs in inner city schools would be an anchor to troubled teens, keeping them off the streets. These programs need not be a financial drain on school systems; they can be self-sustaining through volunteers and fundraisers. Dancing can also improve relationships of married couples. With more adults taking dance classes and ballroom programs being implemented in the high schools, there could be a return of community ballrooms throughout America.

Child or teen, middle-aged or elderly, I hope you discover what I did—to dance is to live!

PART I

Learning to Dance

"If you're one of those people who says
'Life's a bore,' then it's because you're
stupid, and that's all there is to it."

Buzz Champneys

Chapter 1

Dance to Live

The world around me disappeared as the handsome young man in a black tuxedo lifted the elegant woman over his head, making the shape of a 'T.' The music climaxed as he spun. Bringing her down in a twirl, they continued to waltz about the room. I imagined I was at the ball watching Prince Charming and Cinderella.

Could life really be like a fairy tale? Closing my eyes, I dreamed I was in their place.

My thirteen-year-old heart pounded as I watched the traveling university ballroom dance company perform at a community college just outside Pacifica, California where I lived—a town on the coast, just south of San Francisco. My parents had taken our family to see the show, and I was overwhelmed at the exhibition of the students as they did the quickstep, tango, and foxtrot around the floor. A wild swing number with athletic lifts had us pulsing in our seats.

"Wouldn't you like to dance like those young people?" My father woke me from my reverie.

"Oh, Dad, do you think I ever could?" I responded.

"Sure, why not? I would love to see you do the same thing in college," he admitted.

Throughout my young life my father often spoke of his collegiate experiences, joking that he studied hard, but never missed an opportunity to dance with a pretty girl. He continually encouraged his children to pursue higher education and, in that process, get involved in many activities to make it a joyous adventure.

Time passed quickly. I changed a lot in five years. I still had the ivory complexion and baby blue eyes but my flat, skinny frame transformed to a shapely five-foot, eight-inch height. My short, medium-brown hair grew down to the middle of my back in thick, wavy curls.

I graduated from high school, having worked hard in my studies and was accepted to Brigham Young University in Provo, Utah—the home of the best college ballroom dance team in America, the same company that performed near

Pacifica. The school was in the shadow of the majestic Wasatch Mountain range. It was a large private university with a student body of 26,000.

After my plane landed in Salt Lake City, I caught a shuttle that drove me the forty-five minutes south to Provo and found myself awestruck at the grandiose peaks lining the highway. My eyes lifted to the huge letter Y painted brilliantly on the mountain backdrop. Inspiration and gratitude pierced my heart as we came upon the school entrance with the words boldly outlined, "Enter to Learn, Go Forth to Serve." I couldn't believe I was finally here.

In 1977 little experience was necessary to get into the BYU ballroom dance program. At the tryout, we were each asked to pin a number on our back and follow a young teacher in doing basic dance steps. Mostly they wanted to see if we had rhythm and the ability to learn quickly. They would teach us the rest. After the judges watched us for a short while, they deliberated and handed a list to the teacher. She announced some numbers, mine included, and asked us to join her on the other side of the room. The rest were dismissed.

"Congratulations on making it into the ballroom dance program," the teacher said with a smile. My heart leaped and noises of delight echoed around me. "You will first need to sign up for the Standard Bronze class. Standard dances include slow waltz, foxtrot, tango, quickstep, and Viennese waltz. In succeeding semesters you will take the Silver class, followed by a Gold class. The director will decide if you are good enough for the backup team and eventually the touring team."

"If any of you are interested in Latin dancing, you can sign up for those classes as well. You are all invited to a dance lab that will be held tomorrow evening. It is a chance for those in the dance program to use the skills they have acquired. I know you haven't learned much yet, but you still might like to attend. Again, congratulations and welcome into the program."

The next night when I walked into the main campus ballroom, I found a carousel of swirling couples with strides that took them across the floor in what seemed like only a few steps. Big band music invited me in. I was mesmerized and fascinated at the supreme posture of the couples with heads extended like they were in another sphere. Not caring if anyone asked me to dance, I was content to watch the drama.

Soon a familiar girl approached. She was a very pretty blond, with hair feathered and curled in a popular 70's style. Her smile was infectious as she introduced herself, "Hi, I'm Sandy. We tried out together, didn't we?"

"Yes, I'm Alexis. Can you believe this?"

"It's incredible!" Sandy replied, watching the colorful movement.

I couldn't keep the passion bottled up any longer and blurted out, "THIS IS WHAT I WANT TO DO! I WANT TO BE A GREAT DANCER!" speaking half to her, half to myself.

"I feel exactly the same way," she returned with sincerity, her face in a trance-like state.

No one asked us to dance that night, but we left lit up by a flame—a flame we hoped would lead us to our goal, like that held by a torchbearer running for the Olympics.

In our beginning class we quickly discovered that we were to learn the fine art of International Style dancing, a method used in all the national and international competitions. It was considered the premier art form. There was no breaking apart from one's partner in this technique and involved learning to move as one. Our instructors began educating us in the slow waltz and quickstep.

The first day of class my teacher said, "If you want to become good at dancing, make up your mind to wake early and practice from six to eight before school, in addition to class time. We also have a competition every Wednesday night between all those in our program, according to level. This is to give you experience and encourage you to improve yourselves."

Increasing my ability was top priority to me, so I committed myself to the extra effort. Finding an eager partner in my class with the same goals, we met together in the early hours. He was a slender, good-looking freshman who, to my relief, just wanted to keep our relationship a friendship.

Our classes and practices were always held in Room 134 of the Stephen L. Richards building. The well-lit area was the size of a basketball court, minus the hoops, with a single row of chairs lining the perimeter. A quality sound system was provided, and mirrors covered one long wall to help us perfect our moves.

Feeling awkward when I first started, I knew my steps were too small and my topline needed help, the topline being the connection with one's partner, as well as the position of arms and head. Our teacher told the girls that if our feet were stepped on, it was our own fault. We hadn't gotten out of the way for the man to take his required steps. My toes were tromped on often.

More technique was involved than I ever imagined with so much to assimilate at once—landing on a heel or toe at just the right time, maintaining hip contact with my partner, and keeping arms and head in perfect position. Slowly, however, I began to progress. At the end of the semester we took a standardized performing exam administered by professionals from a dance association and received our Bronze medal. It was nerve-wracking, but my partner and I did admirably.

The next semester I moved into the Silver ballroom class. Very quickly a young man in my group asked me to be his partner for competitions, and we rehearsed many mornings before school. Ecstatic when we achieved second place in the Silver waltz competition early in the semester,

I wrote to inform my parents and received the following communication from my father, which he dictated on a cassette tape for me. It was his way to have the long conversation he wanted with a minimal cost:

Dear Alexis,

I was so thrilled to hear about you winning second place in the waltz. If you love to dance, honey, concentrate on dance for the one wonderful opportunity to go to Europe, or wherever, with the dancing team. Five years from now, could you buy that experience? Could you work for three years, and put the money down, and say, "Here, I want to buy that experience?" Of course you couldn't. If the time or opportunity presents itself, do it; because it won't come again. It only happens once. Just once. And if you aren't brave enough, courageous enough, wise or adventurous enough to take advantage of the things that present themselves, then you just kind of exist in life. You don't really live.

And maybe I'm foolish—a foolish old man. But Jiminy Christmas! Today my tennis partner didn't show up, so wow, I had the funnest time running I've had in a long time. And I was absolutely exhausted when I finished running. But I sure had fun. And tomorrow I'm going flying. I stopped and thought, *Gee, I had fun with my friend, Skip, the other day flying, so I'd better give old Skip a call.* And so old Skip and I are going flying together tomorrow and see if we can't scare the daylights out of each other.

You just have to look for the bright side. I don't mean life is all play. But if you don't make life interesting, if you're one of those people who says "Life's a bore," then it's because you're stupid, and that's all there is to it. Life, at no matter what age, can be full and exciting. Remember, just thoroughly enjoy yourself. Keep smiling. Live, honey! Dance to live.

I loved my dad for his advice and example. I didn't know anyone who lived life more fully than my father. He had worked hard to receive his private pilot license a couple of years earlier. I imagined all his youthful escapades with a laugh, like the sword fighting scene he choreographed for a college play and the water shows he put on as a recreation director, where he would dive into a gasoline-covered pool with his cape aflame. "Adventurous" was Dad through and through. I appreciated his support and encouragement in something I had already decided myself.

Athletic and fun loving, my father, was a tall, dark and handsome type who danced me around our living room to Frank Sinatra when I was growing up. I got my baby blue eyes from Dad. He loved to talk about his courting days in the '40s when he and my mother danced to the big bands. He knew the pleasure of it.

My Silver class instructor, a balding law student and previous member of the touring team, continued to teach us slow waltz steps, having us change partners every few minutes. Suddenly I found myself in the arms of a tall, broad-shouldered young man with wavy brown hair and dark blue eyes. Floating across the room together, I thought, *He is so smooth!*

Our teacher, looking for a couple to show what he just taught, pointed to us and said, "You did really well. Let's have you demonstrate that sequence."

While our classmates watched, we danced the whole set perfectly, my face turning red when everyone clapped. Disappointed when the teacher told us to change partners, I made a mental note of my tall discovery for future reference.

A few weeks later my Silver instructor taught us the finer points of the tango by having us do the basic walk in a circle. With my knees bent and legs reaching out in a slight sideways motion, I felt like a tarantula. Moving around the ring and trying out the maneuver with different partners, I came upon Mr. Smooth. "My name is David Beckstead," he said with a smile.

"Hi." My eyes went from his to the floor sheepishly. "Mine is Alexis Champneys."

"Alexis? Mmm, that's a very pretty name. I don't think I will forget that. What are you majoring in?"

"Communications. And you?" I asked.

"Pre-med."

Hmm, pre-med, I pondered. *He must be pretty smart.* We attempted the steps together, and I acknowledged his superiority over the others I had just tested.

"Change partners," proclaimed the teacher. Reluctantly David and I moved apart. I made my way around the circle feeling very awkward with the other boys. Then David Beckstead appeared again, making an impression by remembering my uncommon name.

After class Sandy approached and said, "The tango is really hard and different from the waltz or quickstep."

"Yeah," I agreed. "Did you dance with David Beckstead? He is so smooth. He has a nice feel to him."

"True," remarked my blond friend. "He's not wiry and tense like some of these guys. I danced with one boy who reminded me of a Mack truck."

She looked at me sideways. "If you are getting any ideas about David, you better forget it. I hear he has a steady girlfriend."

"Oh," I let out dejectedly. "Anyone would be better than the guy I'm dancing with now for competition."

I turned to look across the room at my partner. He waved and yelled, "Hey, Alexis, I'll see you in the morning for practice."

"Sure," I responded with mock enthusiasm.

"Why are you dancing with him anyway?" Sandy asked.

"I didn't want to hurt his feelings."

Chapter 2

The Partner of My Dreams

My Silver competition partner had glasses and a rather nerdish demeanor with a smile that reminded me of a chipmunk. He was overconfident in his abilities as a dancer, and it annoyed me that he took my hand each time as if he had won a great prize. We did fine when we first started competing. But as we learned more technique, he misinterpreted it, taking each step as if he were trying to sit, forcing me into the strangest posture. I could not keep hip contact with him as required and had to sway my back to get close enough. I flinched every time I saw our reflection in the mirrors. Frustration and embarrassment came over me at the competitions when I noticed the strange looks people gave us as we passed them.

Near the end of the semester after class one day, my instructor took me aside and questioned, "What happened to your dancing, Alexis? You can do much better than that."

"Wait here," he said as he walked over to the sound cabinet to put on an elegant waltz tune. Then taking my right hand in his left and putting his other arm around my back, he danced me around the room with supreme posture to the three-count beat, showing me first how to lower, then extend each step only closing at the end of the third beat. It was heaven. My teacher was a superior, experienced dancer and I followed like a champ. A glimpse in the mirrors gave proof of my potential. The swooping highs and lows made me feel like a yacht surging a wavy sea. When the music stopped, my instructor complimented me. "Very good. Now *that's* how to waltz."

My confidence was renewed. But where, oh, where was the partner who could help me achieve my dream?

The next semester I found myself in the Gold technique class. Some students had dropped out of the program, and I was relieved to find my Silver partner was one of them. The class, which included the touring team members, opened up an opportunity for me to dance with veterans and I was very happy about it.

Having made it to the Gold class meant I was now on the backup team and given the chance to participate in a few local performances. I was getting closer to a coveted position on the touring team—my dream. Over the past months at early-morning practices, I watched the touring members rehearse at the other end of the room in awe. Their skills were superb, inspiring me to work even harder. We now had to attend a team class, as well as one for technique. Our teacher for both classes was the director of the whole dance program, Emerson Lyman.

In our backup class, Mr. Lyman worked with us on performing numbers. In the technique class we learned competition routines while trading partners often.

Two months into technique class Mr. Lyman announced, "It is now time to permanently pair up with someone with whom you would like to take the medals exam. Gentlemen, choose a partner that is compatible. You will work with this person for the rest of the semester."

"Great, just great," I said sarcastically leaning over to Sandy. "Here it comes. Someone with no natural talent will ask me, and I will be back where I started, picking up bad posture and poor habits. Oh, I'll never get anywhere!"

Sandy gave me a sympathetic smile, just as a competent young man whispered in her ear. She nodded and walked away with him. *Well, at least she has a good partner*, I told myself.

Suddenly, there was a tap on my shoulder and I turned to see Jeremy Stocks. Over six-feet tall with dark hair and eyes, Jeremy was not bad to look at. He smiled. "Alexis, would you like to be my dance partner?"

Shocked, my thoughts went wild, *Jeremy Stocks!? Jeremy is asking me to dance with him?*

Jeremy had been in the ballroom dance program at BYU for over four years and was a member of the touring team. I think he delayed his graduation by changing his major a few times just so that he could dance longer. From our exchanges in class, I knew he was graceful and heavenly to take the floor with.

"I'd love to be your partner, Jeremy." Love was not the right word. I felt like I was blasting off in the rocket ride at the local amusement park.

I tried to get over the shock in my mind, *Jeremy Stocks asked me to be his partner. I don't believe it. Of all the girls he could dance with who have more experience, he is asking me!*

Once paired up, we were free to practice our routines. Jeremy took me into dance position and we were off. I was on cloud nine. How could dancing be so beautiful? He was one of the smooth ones. With fabulous, old-time music playing, we circled the room in elongated steps, moving in perfect unison, flying on eagle's wings.

It took me back to my first experience with flight in the second grade. My mother had signed me up for a community ballet class that ran for three months after school. After teaching the basics, my instructor told us to pretend we were butterflies and move any way we desired. I leaped and waved my arms to Tchaikovsky as though I were in love with the air, feeling the exhilaration of flinging my body through space. The same thrill returned in the arms of Jeremy.

Rehearsing with Jeremy was a whole new experience, since he knew how to lower and extend better than any young man I had matched up with before. His movements helped me feel each dance. I just followed and marvelous things happened.

His expertise was particularly important to me in learning the tango. The tango is very awkward at first, because the woman must slightly turn her body and step behind herself with a staccato motion as she moves backwards. It never felt right before. But Jeremy had the basic movement down to a science and I only had to conform. It was exhilarating. Previously, I never appreciated the dance. With Jeremy as my partner, the tango became my passion, and I threw my whole effort into head snaps, whiplashing my hair behind me.

Jeremy and I rehearsed each morning before school to increase our proficiency, as well as the hour in technique class.

Meanwhile, in my backup team rehearsals we were learning a medley of five different Standard dances. My main partner for the number was a nice enough guy, but he had very little confidence and struggled with the steps. My worst challenge was dealing with his terrible morning breath, the result of his not eating breakfast.

One morning after I tore a piece of chewing gum in half and offered part to him, he said, "Ever since we've been on the backup team you've been giving me gum. Do you think I have bad breath?"

"Oh, no," I quickly replied. "I just want to share." I turned away and rolled my eyes. I had hoped he would get the hint, but he was pretty dense. I continued to offer him gum.

My favorite part of the medley was when I did a twirl into the arms of David Beckstead. We floated around for a few measures, and then I regretfully spun back to my original partner with the dragon breath. Each time I danced with

David, I found myself saying words in my head like *smooth, solid, nice.*

In the technique class David had chosen Kathy as a partner. She wasn't the prettiest girl, but her sweet personality and grace made up for it. I was impressed that he sought her out, because it showed character. He could see her true value as a talented dancer and kind person. Hearing that David still had his girlfriend, I put him on my "taken" list.

Chapter 3

Surprises

The day I had dreamed of for years had finally come—my first performance as a member of the BYU Ballroom Dance Company. The backup team was to do a number for the floorshow of a local church dance. In preparation we were taught the requirements for make-up.

I arrived early at the church with the other girls where we busied ourselves in getting ready for the performance. Leaning close to the mirror, I complained, "My eyes look so freaky with this dark eyeliner and bright blue eye shadow."

Sandy squinted. "It is so hard to get these false eyelashes on straight," she said.

"I guess they want us to wear this stuff so our eyes stand out from far away," another friend suggested.

"Yeah, but we are not very far away in this building," commented Sandy.

After dressing, I sat on a couch in the foyer and enjoyed the fluffy fabric of my costume as it billowed about me, even if it was a hand-me-down from the touring team. Waiting for the exciting moment to go on, I reminisced on my first, serious dance class years ago and how far I had come.

When I was thirteen years old, the boys in eighth grade called me a "beanpole." I lacked confidence but not enthusiasm for life. Although I had taken a ballet class for a couple of months in second grade, I hadn't done any dancing until I reached junior high. I don't know why my mother's friend, Sue Jensen, asked me to join her ballet class that year, but I was always glad I did, for I discovered my wings again.

As a newcomer, I acknowledged the superior dance ability of the older girls. But that didn't intimidate me. My desire to learn motivated me to give my best effort as I tried to do spins and twirls like Margot Fonteyn. Looking back, I know I was not good, but in my thirteenth year I thought I was and so continued to dance.

At fifteen I was anxious for one of the biggest events my church had for teenagers — the Dance Festival. The Church of Jesus Christ of Latter-day Saints was established in the early 1800's. Because of religious persecution, the members were forced to move west to the Salt Lake Valley where they could have religious freedom. On the long trek across the plains, their leader, Brigham Young, told them to dance in the evenings to find release from the toils of the day and to rejoice in God. Dancing has ever since been included in our activities.

The capable person put in charge of the Dance Festival was Susan Jensen, my ballet instructor. Sue had her own studio and also taught jazz, tap, and ballroom dancing. She was like a goddess to me, a five-nine slender, graceful beauty. Her dark hair was always perfectly coifed like a 1960s Miss America. In her teens she had performed with Ballet West, a professional ballet troupe in Utah, but said she was too tall to be a ballerina any longer. Her commanding presence and fast-moving, teaching style kept everyone's interest, and I idolized her.

One day Sue called me on the phone and said, "I am putting together a ballet specialty number for the festival. It will have twelve dancing princesses. Please come to the tryouts. I think you will be right for it."

Pleased to have her vote of confidence, I showed up willingly and was delighted when I became one of the twelve dancing princesses in the festival that year.

My church had a youth group in every town in the San Francisco Bay area that learned the same set of dances. At the end of the year, the youth in the region performed on a college football field. Our final show involved all the youth in my church of northern California, and it was held in the Oakland Coliseum.

Imagine two thousand teenagers moving to the swing, polka, Charleston, square dance, or waltz in beautiful costumes. It was thrilling and I loved being part of it.

My senior year of high school Sue Jensen asked me and my sister Karrie to help teach the other youth groups for the regional Dance Festival. We were happy to help. Karrie, a sophomore at the time, studied the girls' parts and I learned the boys' steps. We grew in skill by working with Sue and had a ball getting to know the other teenagers. Our monthly church dances were better than ever because Karrie and I knew everyone who attended, and we never lacked for partners. My sister and I grew to be closer friends in the process. Dance Festivals made our high school years exciting and inspired me to continue dancing in college.

"Are you ready to dance?" asked Sandy, bringing me back to reality.

"I sure am," I replied, taking my position. Dressed like a princess, I was going out in front of those people as part of the college team I had once aspired to, making my dreams come true.

Although I was very nervous as we entered the floor, the music swept me up in what I loved to do. Soon, however, our formation moved too close to the audience. I was taken into a dip, and without any warning found myself eye to eye with a twelve-year-old boy who exclaimed loudly, "Ew, sick!"

He was not impressed with my bright blue eye shadow and false eyelashes either. Here I was bedecked, trained, and blown up like a champion, only to have my bubble popped by a juvenile. The comment shook me but I continued on the best I could. Later I was able to laugh about it in the hall with my teammates. My first performance with the BYU Ballroom Company did not turn out anything like I had imagined.

Dancing was like that—full of surprises. Sometimes the longed-for, perfect spin around the floor ended up the perfect disaster. On my way back to my apartment, I reminisced on one such instance with my dad. Every year when our church held a special family ball, each senior girl had the first dance with her father.

My senior year I looked forward to taking the floor with Dad, and I wore a new dress for the occasion. When the special moment came, Dad and I moved nervously to a beautiful foxtrot in front of hundreds of people observing from the sides. As the tune approached its conclusion, I thought he was taking me into one of his dramatic dips which we had done at many other balls, so I flung myself into it with great force. Only he was not planning a dip at all. My weight threw him off balance, and he staggered forward several feet, tripping awkwardly trying to keep me from falling — all very undignified and embarrassing.

Another surprise materialized shortly after my first performance with the backup team at. It took place at BYU's girls' choice dance called "Preference." I had dated a tall, good-looking guy named Brad about three times that semester. He had a mustache, dark hair, and a wonderful physique, besides being kind and polite. I definitely wanted to continue seeing him. So, I invited him to be my date for the dance, explaining that I would have to leave him for a short time in the middle so I could perform with the backup team during the floorshow. He was okay with that and said he was excited to see my number. Unfortunately, when we arrived at the ballroom, I could tell that he was extremely uneasy about dancing with me. I tried every way possible to get him to relax, complimenting him on his leading and telling him he was a good dancer, which he was.

With trepidation he said, "I should be brave and try more steps. You follow so well. I probably could do just about anything while dancing with you."

That made me feel good, but Brad still couldn't loosen up.

After I got into my costume for the floorshow, Wayne Cluff, a good friend on the backup team, pulled me aside. "Alexis, we have to come back tomorrow on Saturday night to perform again for the second night of Preference. What do you say we both meet here early and dance together before the performance?"

"I'd like to, Wayne. That would be fun."

I found Brad after our number, and he complimented me on the show. Unfortunately, my exhibition only seemed to increase his apprehension when we danced, but there was nothing I could do about it. Nonetheless, I really liked Brad and hoped he would ask me out again.

I honestly felt that dance ability was not a vital necessity in a future mate. It would be a nice plus, but it certainly wouldn't be the deciding factor.

The next evening Wayne, a friendly guy about my height, unveiled his versatility. Having intense Latin training, he lead me around the floor in a powerful way, turning rock songs into a samba or cha-cha, getting me to do more exciting moves than I had ever done before. While dancing the swing, I felt like a circus flyer. Wayne's ingenuity and talent in leading made my capabilities soar! We didn't want to waste a minute to rest.

As more and more people arrived, unexpectedly I saw Brad, my date from the previous night. A pretty blond was holding his arm. Obviously, she had asked him to the second night of Preference. Jealousy rose up inside of me like mist from a hot spring.

He's in big demand, I thought to myself resentfully.

Brad looked at me, embarrassed. Heat came into my cheeks as well, for there I was with another date. I could understand Brad not wanting to turn down the girl when asked, but he probably wondered how many men I preferred. I wanted to explain that Wayne and I were dancing because we were just passing the time before we had to perform, but I never got the chance.

In examining the situation, I concluded that although Wayne wasn't as tall or handsome as Brad, I had more fun with Wayne. He was easy to talk to and we could be ourselves with each other. We were good buddies. No tension. Suddenly, I didn't care anymore if Brad saw me with Wayne.

Brad didn't ask me out again and I never forgot the euphoric evening I spent with Wayne. The Preference dance turned out to be quite a surprise. There were more surprises to come.

Chapter 4

First Date

It was common for many of the world's best dancers to come to Brigham Young University to teach. One day Emerson Lyman gave the backup team the option of attending the tour group's Saturday session with visiting professionals—the Sextons. It was not mandatory, but we were welcome.

Several backup dancers were mulling around when I showed up, David Beckstead being one of them. He came over to me and asked if I would be his partner for the class.

David was six-foot-one, and for a girl of my height in heels, it was just right. I could not ignore his broad shoulders, muscular build, or his good looks even if he were "taken." As we stepped into closed position, I noted how nicely we fit together.

The focus of the lesson was the quickstep, which is like a fast foxtrot, but more like running than walking. One sequence they taught went like this: run, 2, 3, 4, step hop, step hop, kick, kick, kick, kick, step, leap, slide. We executed the run in promenade, meaning closed position but sideways movement. It was so much fun, and we did it over and over again trying to achieve "oneness" to get it right.

At the end of the session, David thanked me for working with him and expressed his pleasure in dancing with me. I returned the same sentiments.

A day or two later I was sitting down in the school practice room taking off my dance shoes when David Beckstead sat down next to me. "Will you go to the Arts Ball with me?" he questioned. "I decided to ask the prettiest girl I know."

How do you turn down a line like that? I thought. Actually, I was dating a lot then—not the same guy, but many. I did not really like any of them, though. David's charming invitation was hard to resist.

"Sure, but I thought you had a girlfriend."

"Oh, we broke up," David said. "The dance is on St. Patrick's Day in two weeks. We will have to work this date around our performance that same evening. First, we will go to dinner, perform at the church dance, and then attend the Arts Ball afterward."

"I'd like that." I answered.

I never expected David to ask me out. He had seemed uninterested in me up until now, and he was so dedicated to his partner, Kathy. *Was he just asking me out on the rebound from being dumped by his girlfriend?* I wondered.

At our next backup-team rehearsal, Mr. Lyman gathered us around, and said, "I'd like to have a specialty number for our upcoming performance. Would any of you be interested in choreographing and performing a waltz solo?"

I immediately ran over to David, held onto his arm, and pleaded, "Oh, please do it with me. We know enough steps."

He hesitated, a little unsure of himself, then swallowed. "I'm willing if you are."

"Great!" I exclaimed. For a year and a half I had seen soloists practicing in the dance room and longed to be one of them. David went over to Mr. Lyman and volunteered.

The next day when David showed up at my apartment to take me to our solo rehearsal, he was not driving a typical poor-college-student, second-hand car. He opened the door of a new silver, GM Cutlass Supreme. "Whoa," I thought. "This guy has money."

After helping me into the red interior, he put in an 8-track, and we traveled to beautifully orchestrated music. Most of the boys I dated played "Saturday Night Fever." I was impressed with his choice of music, but also the fact that he chose a family vehicle rather than an impractical sporty model.

As we collaborated on our choreography, we formed an introduction, combined some old routines, threw in a few lifts, and set the ending. We rehearsed every morning and evening. Waltzing with David was very romantic.

When the night of our date came, I was full of nervous excitement. David drove me to a restaurant, where we enjoyed conversation over dinner.

"So tell me more about yourself, David."

"Well, I told you I was raised on a cattle farm south of Preston, Idaho. Preston is a small town of 3,700 just north of the Utah border. My parents have eight children—four boys and four girls. I am the oldest son. I do a lot of work for my dad—planting, cutting and bailing hay, and harvesting grain. I fed cows in the winter while I was growing up.

"My father and mother both have a college education and tried to teach me the importance of it. My father is a part-time veterinarian also. I told you already that I want to become a family doctor. So, what about you?"

I took my turn. "My parents grew up in the Utah area, but they both received their college education in California. They liked it so much they decided to stay. I am the third of six children, spending most of my growing up years in Pacifica, California, which is just south of San Francisco. My father, a high school teacher, did not have much money to help us with our education, so I work part-time as a secretary in the Physics Department typing papers and tests for the professors to make my own way. I enjoy it. I hope my Communications major will help me get a job in a personnel department, since I like working with people."

Interested in his latest relationship, I ventured, "You used to have a girlfriend. Do you mind if I ask what happened?"

"She wanted to break up. I guess she lost interest in me. I call her 325. I have a code name for each girl that I've filed before in my life and that is her file number."

I giggled at the thought of him having 325 girlfriends.

He broke down, "Well, okay, so it was actually her apartment number."

I giggled again.

Following dinner we drove to our performance in Orem — a town bordering Provo. The other girls and I hurriedly dressed, applied our makeup, and pinned on a curly hairpiece about the size of a large soup bowl. David and I enjoyed dancing our Standard medley with the team, but we noticed that one girl did not.

The inevitable surprise made its entrance on cue. During the number, much to my friend's vexation, her hairpiece came undone at the top, and it did some creative flapping as she moved. It looked like a pot hanging on a tree waiting for maple syrup to drip into it. The audience chortled at the scene. She was in tears by the end of the performance and expressed her extreme embarrassment in the hall. David leaned over to me and whispered, "Some people found it great entertainment."

When we took the floor to begin our solo, I was struck with panic and forgot parts of our routine completely. Luckily, I could still follow and David very calmly led me through memory lapses. While my face showed anxiety, David, on the other hand, had a beautiful smile the whole way through. I was relieved when it was finally over, disillusioned that my long-anticipated solo had not turned out as I had hoped.

In the hall I begged David's forgiveness, but he brushed it off as nothing, pulling out a gorgeous, white orchid corsage like a promise of lovelier things ahead.

The Arts Ball was a semi-formal affair held in the Harris Fine Arts Center on campus. The main level had a large open area with an orchestra playing at one end, alternating with a jazz band spewing out tunes on the opposite side. Above, three balconies circled the open center floor. We climbed the stairs to the less-crowded top balcony and danced the Viennese waltz up and down the corridors as though we were in Vienna on New Years' Eve.

We also tried our best at dances like the tango, quickstep and swing. It was unusual for me to go to a social dance with an expert guide, and I reveled in it.

A few of our ballroom friends were there going crazy. Couples that usually won our weekly competitions created a stir with their expertise. We gave each other knowing looks.

Partway through the evening we posed for pictures, me in a baby blue gown that matched my eyes and David in a classy suit. We danced until midnight. It was an impressive first date.

An incident occurred in the fall of the previous semester that made me react very hesitatingly when David took me home to my apartment. I had a proposal of marriage by a young man I dated only a month. I knew he was not for me and turned him down, but it made me very wary of jumping into a relationship too soon. My goal was to live life to the fullest, considering marriage to be down the road a ways for me, not in the near future. You might say I was "gun shy."

When David and I approached my door that night, I did not give him a chance to get friendly. Thanking him for the nice evening, I slipped quickly into my living room wondering how it would affect him.

As it turned out, my rapid exit didn't discourage him. It may have had the opposite effect, for he asked me to a movie the next week.

When he picked me up for our date, not wanting him to think I was totally cold, I slid in to sit in the middle of the seat. While driving, I took immediate notice of a beautifully orchestrated song he was playing called "Laura." The sweet strains of the violins had a magical effect upon me. Was this part of a strategy?

We had a nice time watching the movie. As usual, conversation with him was interesting and easy. I was surprised, however, upon returning to his silver car to find the movable armrest in the front seat all the way down making it impossible to sit near him. *Uh oh*, I thought. *He must only want to be friends. Obviously he doesn't want me near him.*

That night I made up my mind not to make any move until he did. I would play it his way.

Chapter 5

Dancing in the Dark

Mr. Lyman had been nagging Jeremy to stop moving his left arm erratically. "You're not driving a bus, Jeremy. Keep that arm still."

Although Jeremy was very smooth, he often forgot to keep his topline solid. It did not bother me. I made the decision long before not to criticize my dance partner, and it had served me well. It had served me especially well when instances arose where I perceived the problem to lie with my partner but the teacher told me I was at fault. It was safer to keep my judgments to myself.

Finally, at one practice Jeremy said, "Alexis, I am going to ruin your medal exam score. I will have you dance with me when I am tested, but maybe you better find someone else to do your medal exam with you."

No matter what I said in opposition, he was adamant that I find another partner. I knew who I wanted my partner to be. After class I walked over to David Beckstead, explained my situation, and asked, "Would you mind doing my dance test with me?"

"Sure, I'd be happy to, but we had better practice together. Let's meet at the Student Center Ballroom tonight at seven."

It was all arranged. We met and found an empty practice room upstairs next to the busy ballroom, but the light switch eluded us. The only illumination came from the hall radiating through a single, miniature pane in the door, which was not much. Upon giving up our search for the light, David said, "Well, we can still dance in the dark."

"Sure, why not?" I agreed. We slipped into our shoes, turned on our tape recorder, and began to go through our routines. At this point David and I had improved so remarkably by dancing with our regular partners that by the time we got together we had mastered many problems.

First, we ran as "one" to the four-count beat of the quickstep—lively, fast and fun. Moves like the hairpin turn, scoops, and the four-quick run left us out of breath.

The dramatic tango was full of passion, pivoting one way then reversing into flicks and head snaps with my hair flying.

Next was the waltz. As we lowered and reached highs together, it became clear that it was our best dance. By this time our bodies glistened from perspiration.

Throughout, my mind wandered. This was the epitome of romance—moving in perfect synchronization with a masculine man to beautiful music in the dark. Was he touched by the mood as well? What was he thinking?

At the start of the foxtrot, I stole a glance at him. His serene face told me he was savoring the experience. We glided across the room in euphoria, our muscles toned from months of practice.

I loved the smell of his cologne, touching his brawny arm, and settling into his right side. I was vividly aware of his thighs rubbing against mine. As our practice time concluded, we looked at each other with new intimacy. He did not try to kiss me, but I wondered if he thought about it.

As we left the dark room, he confided that International Style foxtrot was his favorite dance. Was it because the motion never stopped like it did with other rhythms? Or that it mimicked a light bird in a wind draft floating effortlessly through space?

The next important event to come up was the International Ball, a major competition sponsored by the dance department at the end of every semester to find the top dancers at Brigham Young University. Over the past year the same three or four experienced couples placed in the Standard finals over and over again. Beating them seemed impossible.

I called David and asked for a ride. Since he had already arranged to bring his dance partner, Kathy, he escorted two women. He picked me up looking very handsome in a tuxedo his grandmother had bought for him.

During the evening David competed with Kathy, while I partnered with Jeremy. General dancing was intermixed, and David took turns with his two ladies. As we visited in the ballroom, I was amazed that Kathy never acted jealous or unkind to me. She had every reason to. On the contrary, she seemed willing to share her partner, which made me really like her. Later she announced to us that she would not be enlisting with the team for fall semester because of a required internship.

Immediately after the ball, David dropped off Kathy at her apartment. On the way home to my place he ventured, "Well, with Kathy out of the picture and Jeremy graduating, how would you like to be my dance partner next September when we are on the touring team?"

I couldn't believe how easily our present partners exited the picture. I replied, "I'd love to, David," relieved that my future in dance was well taken care of.

Arriving at my apartment and unwilling to have the evening end, I said. "My sister made me a cake for my birthday, which is tomorrow. Would you like to come in and have some, David?"

"Thank you, I'd like that. Your birthday is tomorrow?"

"Yes."

"But that's April 1st — April Fools' Day."

"It sure is."

"That's funny," said David. "You won't believe this, but my mother's birthday is on April Fools' Day, too."

"Incredible."

David seemed glad that he didn't have to leave. Entering my living quarters, it seemed almost too convenient that my roommates and sister Karrie had gone to bed. As we ate our dessert, David shared his goals and ambitions, his philosophy on affecting people for good, and the great ideals of life. When I looked at the clock, I was surprised it was two in the morning. Time had flown. I never felt this at ease with other men I dated. Talking had never been more comfortable—no pretense, no straining to find the words to say. It was as though I had known David all my life.

The next day I received a beautiful bouquet of flowers from my dancing man. He kept chalking up the points.

In our dance exams we did very well and were proud to receive our Gold medals. It represented a great deal of work, hours, and effort. However, we were still vividly aware that we had a long way to go to reach the level of the professionals we admired. The gap made us want to continue our progress.

I diverted any physical affection with David, wanting dance to be our focus. When school ended, David went back to Idaho to work on the family farm, and I went home to the Bay area to work as a temporary secretary. I sent him an enlarged picture of us dancing together that someone snapped at a performance, which triggered occasional phone calls from him. I looked forward to those calls like a child to Christmas morning.

During one conversation, I told him that I was practicing our ballroom routines in my garage every night, wearing out my heels on the cement floor. My biggest problem was avoiding the huge center beam. One night I bashed into it, bruising my shoulder.

Something pivotal happened during those workouts—I captured the feeling of how to step backward, keeping my feet out of the way of the man better than I had ever done before. It was a skill that would make the difference in my dancing thereafter.

David also sent occasional letters, giving me insight into the farm life, and he always included a bit of philosophy. One day I received the following:

Dear Alexis,

I really enjoyed talking to you last evening. I guess I ought to call you more often.

Well, sit back, relax and I'll tell you about all the exciting jobs I did today. This morning I hauled one load of hay and took it out to the cattle auction my Dad owns so the yardman could feed the cows. Then I came home and had a bowl of wheat mush for breakfast. (I always like to work for about one hour or so before I eat breakfast, so I will work up an appetite.) After breakfast I took my brother and went to rescue a tractor I drove into a big mud hole and got stuck. It was stuck Saturday and my dad was uptight because I'm not smart enough, yet, to stay away from mud holes. My dad wanted me to get it unstuck Saturday, but after his big lecture I made him wait an extra day.

The rest of the day I used the loader tractor to move dirt, hay and straw around so I could prepare places to dump the second crop hay. As usual, it was so hot that I almost fried my poor old body. Anyway, I survived another day and made some improvements on the farm, which will make tomorrow easier.

One sad thing happened this afternoon. The tape player ate that Henry Mancini tape I was telling you about. I'm heart broken! All those mellow foxtrots gone. I'm going to perform an operation on the tape to see if I can save it.

Part of last night's phone conversation with you caused me to think about, and refine today a thought that has been running through my mind lately. I've been trying to gain a better understanding of what it is in a person that causes him to improve his life. I've long maintained that external force isn't the answer. Improvement should be maintained from within a person and not from outside pressures. (Granted, external help can make a difference, but it isn't the best way to cause a person to change.) Why is it that we go on a self-improvement program for a little while only later to lose interest and stop? Because our desires are externally motivated. If we can truly clear away the clouds and implant good desires upon ourselves, then we have won the battle and the prize of true joy is ours.

I'm tired. I'm going to bed. I've enjoyed writing this letter to you. Have fun. Enjoy the rest of the summer. Good luck at work and enjoy some moments of your own. Take a week off and go to your family cabin. Don't run into the post in your garage!

I got a kick out of my farmer's homespun conversation and outlook. His letters and calls made my summer less tedious.

September came before I knew it, and I arrived in Provo a few days before school to begin work in the Physics Department. Since we hadn't arranged to meet at a certain time, I kept wondering when David would show up. After work the second day, I walked toward my apartment in thick traffic, keeping my head down to avoid eye contact with the passersby only looking up after I ran across the street to my apartment building. Standing there was David, leaning against his car smiling with his arms crossed. Something inside of me leaped.

"You look so thin," I observed as I approached.

"I ran a marathon this summer. It made me drop some weight."

"You didn't tell me." I said surprised. I was dumbfounded at his stamina and drive.

"I ran every day all summer and decided to enter at that last minute. I did pretty well. I was able to complete the whole thing and only walked a little at the end."

"Amazing! Do you want to come in and I'll fix you some dinner?"

"Sure."

There was no hug or affection. Both of us were a little unsure of our relationship having been separated for four months. As the evening wore on, we began to relax, with it eventually feeling like old times.

When David didn't linger very long, making some excuse to leave, I thought it was a little strange. "I guess he wants to start out slowly," I contemplated. Anticipating the dancing we'd do, I told myself, *This is going to be a great year!*

The next day we went to our first meeting with Mr. Lyman and the team, and it was wonderful to reunite with friends from last years' backup team, especially Sandy and Wayne. Our colleagues on both teams were friendly, nice-looking kids with fine goals. It was a privilege to rub shoulders with them.

David and I had been trained for the eight-couple Standard team. As it turned out, the shorter students usually ended up dancing Latin. Tall people have a tendency to be better at the slow, graceful moves of the Standard dances, which require those elongated steps. The shorter students seem to be better at the quick movements required in the Latin dances. There are always exceptions, but it was a trend that seemed to follow. We paired up to learn our first routine — a medley of five Standard dances, taught by Mr. Lyman. Of course I danced with my Idahoan.

It was a classic routine with steps that took us into continually changing formations. I especially liked the girls' rippling spins into side-by-side grapevines. We spun back to our partners, waltzing to two lines that moved around into a circle. A change in the music took us into the tango. After head flicks, the women spun out, the men turning the opposite direction to hit a sharp pose. There were lifts and two diagonal lines that wove through each other using the foxtrot. Quickstep hops and runs made us pass through once more. Viennese turns moved us into an ending dip. I looked forward to running through the composition time and time again, and became second nature.

Life as a dancer was demanding and was proving to increase my stamina. At the beginning of the year I slowly walked the 106 stairs from the Richards building that took me up a hill to the plateau of the main campus where I worked, stopping several times to catch my breath. But weeks into the semester, I took pride in the fact that I could run up those monstrous steps without a reprieve, not even feeling winded at the top. Each time I mounted the summit I felt like jumping up and down like Rocky. It was invigorating. My supreme physical condition was the result of intense workouts. Practicing the quickstep to a couple of songs was like running the mile, and I practiced for hours daily.

A mixture of smells was associated with that practice—sweat combined with deodorant and talcum powder, dowsed with men's cologne and ladies perfume. When standing still, it varied, depending on whom I was closest to. While dancing, it was all stirred up like a magical witch's brew that left one wondering if it was a good witch or a bad witch—sometimes pleasant, sometimes not.

The worst smell of all was before and after class when we approached the shoe lockers in the hall, lined with air vents. Whew! There was no doubt about it, feet smelled, and shoes worn every day for hours that had sweaty feet in them left no glowing report.

Although dancing was terrific, it took hard work and discipline to be successful. A typical day began with my alarm going off at five a.m. David picked me up and drove me to school for our six o'clock team practice. At seven a.m. we concentrated on our technique. By eight David would have accompanied me to work where I was a secretary four hours each morning in the Physics Department. My afternoons were spent going to lectures, as well as participating in team and technique classes. Each evening David and I ate dinner at the student center and studied at the library. By nine p.m., my farmer was driving me home, so I could get to bed early. It went on day after day.

When possible, David walked me to class, always insisting on carrying my books and opening doors for me. He was a perfect gentleman, and I loved being treated like a lady. We enjoyed discussing all the things we were learning in our courses, treasuring the knowledge and skills we were gaining in our education. On the weekends we looked forward to attending a show or concert. It was a wonderful life! But there was still much more to learn about my dancing partner.

Becky Haynes, my sewer (front), David Beckstead, Alexis Champneys, Lloyd McCallister, Jan Beeton, David Duke, Sandy Petersen, Randy Newquist Northern California Tour

Chapter 6

Down on the Farm

As David drove me home from studying on campus one evening, he looked over the sprawling metropolitan area and reflected, "I don't know how people can stand to live so close to each other in this huddled mass. I love the wide-open spaces back home, looking over a sea of clover hay or a white barley field rippling in the wind. Thinking of it makes me want to get out of town."

"I'd love to see your farm some time," I daydreamed out loud. "It sounds like a beautiful place."

A light came into his eyes and he sat up taller. "You would? Do you mean that?"

"Yes," I replied, "You talk about your home so often that it makes me curious to see it."

"Why don't we go up to Idaho this weekend then? My dad has been hounding me to help him get the last crop of hay hauled."

"I'd like that," I said with enthusiasm.

"I'll take you around to do chores with me," David announced eagerly. "And we will visit my dad's different farms."

"It's a date!"

The weekend came quickly and I met him with my bag packed. On the drive up to Preston I asked him many questions about his family, town, and farm to prepare myself. When we arrived in front of a modest red brick home, we entered to find his parents reading near the fireplace in their family room. They looked up with friendly smiles, acting cordially when David introduced me. His father had a farmer tan, dark from his nose down, and a white forehead where his cowboy hat had shaded him. I could see both mother and father in David's features.

After visiting a little longer and showing me around the comfortable, older home filled with family pictures, David suggested we go to bed early. He said he planned on getting me up at the crack of dawn.

He wasn't kidding. Before it was light, he knocked on my door—the signal to get up. I jumped out of bed and quickly dressed.

We first walked around the main area surrounding the house, a conglomerate of small buildings and sheds, with the exception of one easily identifiable feature—a big red barn. He showed me a smaller milking barn, calf pens, and the corn silage pit.

After David lubricated a vehicle, we went inside for a breakfast consisting of eggs, bacon, hash browns, and toast with frozen preserves.

I thanked his mother for the delicious breakfast before my host pulled me outside again. I followed him to the strangest contraption I had ever seen—a hay hauler. We climbed in and he drove to a nearby field where he showed me how to run the gadgetry. Squealing with delight, I watched it scoop up the seventy-pound bales with the huge fork and watched them flip into a stack behind the cab.

"Hey, you'd make a pretty good farm girl," he announced.

I laughed. "This is more fun than dancing!"

He seemed surprised, but pleased. He finished up most of the small field himself and then suggested we go for a ride through town. Preston's Main Street had a grand total of one traffic light. As we traveled, he pointed out his favorite fast food place, the one grocery store, and the handful of variety and department stores. It was a quiet, quaint little farming town, and I fell in love with it right away.

He pointed to a brick structure with arches. "There's the newspaper building where they print the *Preston Citizen*. That same place was the home of the Parisiana Ballroom for many years. My parents, grandparents, and all the old timers talk about the days when every Friday and Saturday night young people and adults gathered there to ballroom dance to big band music. It was the town's greatest source of entertainment. People still talk as if it were a golden age. But after the advent of television, it declined. Now it is the home of a publisher and offices."

"Sometimes I wonder if I was born in the wrong era," I reflected out loud. "I would love to have grown up ballroom dancing every weekend."

He nodded in agreement.

At lunchtime we stopped to eat at the Polar Bear—a local hamburger joint. As we worked on a couple of cheeseburgers, an old farmer came in. Recognizing David, he walked up to him and smacked him on the arm, "Hey, how are you Dave? I thought you were going to the Y?"

"I am. I'm just home for the weekend." David stood up and introduced me to the farmer. "This is my dance partner, Alexis Champneys."

The old timer winked as he elbowed David. "Is she *just* your dance partner? Huh?" They both laughed and David's cheeks turned ruddy. The older gentleman smiled at me as he walked away to order. I looked down at my burger sheepishly. That same situation arose several times over the weekend as we ran into more of David's friends. I noticed that these locals did not think twice about speaking their minds.

After lunch he took me five miles south of Preston to a small community called Franklin, population 400. We passed through the town, east toward the mountains and stopped at a lovely stretch of farmland. David got out, walked around the front of the truck, and opened the door for me. He pointed to our destination—a grove of tall leafy trees on a hill at the other end of a harvested field, which sloped upward.

As we walked, I inquired, "How did you first get interested in ballroom dancing, David?"

"There was a man in Preston who had been through the dance program at BYU and became an instructor. His name was Neal Swann. When he moved back here, he started a community ballroom class in the evenings, and my mother encouraged me to attend. As a teenager wanting to feel more comfortable with girls, I decided to go and was surprised at how much I enjoyed it.

By the time I got to college, I wanted to do more dancing, so I tried out for the team."

I listened with interest. We came to a wooden barrier. "We have to cross this fence to get to the trees," he explained.

Before I could make an attempt, he picked me up in his strong arms and began climbing the wooden beams. "But, David, I can do it!"

"Oh, I don't want you to rip your pants."

After handling the fence with ease and setting me down gently on the other side, I sighed at his chivalrous gesture, his strength impressing me. I felt like Jane in a Tarzan movie. We continued walking to the trees, where he invited me to sit and enjoy the grand prospect of the valley before us. What a spectacular view! Cache Valley, extending over fifty miles in length and ten miles in width, was surrounded by the steep Rocky Mountains. The patchwork of the farms below looked like an old-fashioned quilt.

"Beautiful!" I gasped. We sat there in quiet awe.

Soberly David began to open up, "My dream is to bring my wife back here and build a big house overlooking this valley. I want to set up my family practice and raise my children in Preston. I hope to make a difference in the lives of the people who live here."

Thoughtfully I remarked, "It's a wonderful dream, David. I know it will come true some day. You deserve it."

As I looked across the farmland, it reminded me of the green San Joaquin Valley of California where I was born and spent my first years before we moved to the San Francisco Bay area. I also recalled that my father was born and raised just over these mountains, south in Ogden, Utah. Dad spoke often about hiking and camping in the Wasatch Range. It was close to my heritage.

I glanced again at David's handsome profile. His abilities and goals impressed me more and more with each passing day. I liked him. I was attracted to him. But deep inside, I didn't know if he were "the one" for me.

One thing is certain, I spoke in my mind, *whoever marries David Beckstead will be one lucky girl*. Having spent so much time in the mountains, I hadn't felt like a city girl. I had always been more happy and comfortable at our cabin or on our family hiking trips. My eyes scanned the horizon once more—what a gorgeous, yet familiar valley. Why did I feel as if I were coming home?

View of beautiful Cache Valley

Chapter 7

Taking the Lead

A month or so into school, Mr. Lyman called us over to speak to him. "I'd like you to be the captain of the touring team, David, and Alexis to be the co-captain. I am putting you two in charge of the early morning practices. Your job is to help the team improve their weak parts, count out the steps, and keep them working." We agreed to take the positions. Past experience teaching at Dance Festivals gave me confidence.

When David accepted the position as captain of our team, I stood back and watched him display his astonishing leadership qualities. He was another Captain Hornblower. By keeping us moving and encouraging feedback, he made us into a cohesive group. I tried to support David in every way possible, counting out the ladies' parts when necessary.

His sarcastic humor and shocking frankness kept us in stitches. For example, after a lackluster run through at six one morning, he said, "That looked like a dog's breakfast. You varmints can do better than that. Let's try it again."

In October all the college performing groups were to put on a big show called the Homecoming Spectacular. It was to be held in the Marriot Center, a huge indoor arena with seating for 23,000 people, where basketball games, concerts, and forums were also held. The Latin and Standard teams had practices in the mammoth building.

Besides presenting our team numbers, David and I, along with several other couples, were called upon to do a short lift sequence before mirrors on side platforms for the finale number. We stayed up late several nights learning the moves. It was exciting, but the hours began to take their toll.

The night before our performance, after a long rehearsal, I was at my breaking point. On the way home in David's car I expressed my worries over my studies, getting enough sleep, and holding up to do my secretarial work. For the first time, he reached over the armrest and took my hand in his. Immediately as his big, strong hand covered mine, a peaceful calm penetrated my whole body. With David there for me, I felt I could keep going.

After he helped me out of the car at my apartment, I looked up at him with a smile and said, "David, you're a wonderful guy."

The corners of his mouth turned up. He walked me to the door holding my hand but still stayed aloof from the kiss. Determined to wait until he thought the time was right, I held back.

The Homecoming Spectacular was a big success. I loved the sparkly, gold costume and thrilled at being lifted and twirled by my robust man. Earlier in the show when I did a Viennese waltz segment with another partner, someone snapped a picture, which ended up being used in advertising flyers.

A few weeks later the professional, Vernon Brock, came to teach us a Spanish dance he had choreographed where the men twirled capes and the women danced with shawls. It was a privilege to be instructed by him.

After that, professionals from Britain and Australia came to give us help in our technique class. My heart palpitated at their superlative demonstrations. David and I took private lessons from these visitors, increasing our skills. Such opportunities made participation in the ballroom program a first-class experience.

One Wednesday evening in November, we went to the school dance competition as usual, but for some reason we were stressed out that day and did not do very well. It was discouraging. David was discontented and seemed to have something on his mind. After the competition, we walked to his car in the dark. After we got in, he did not start the car right away, letting a moment of silence pass before he said, "There are times I feel very lonely when I am with you."

Shocked and hurt, I scratched my head trying to figure out exactly what he meant. I had tried in every way possible to be a good friend to him. Not knowing what to say, I sat quiet.

"Well, aren't you going to say anything?" he asked.

"No," I announced. "You say something."

At that point he lifted the armrest and demanded, "Get over here and sit by me."

Relieved, I started to laugh. "Oh, that's what you are talking about. I thought you didn't want me to sit by you because you always left the arm rest down." I snuggled over next to him.

"I've always hated myself for forgetting to put the arm rest up after the Arts Ball," he confessed.

He did not try anything else that night. The adjustment seemed to pacify him. The stress was relieved, making life good again. Sitting in the middle was much better.

"Who would like to do a lift routine?" Mr. Lyman asked in class. "I need three couples." I looked at David with pleading eyes.

"Let's do it," David responded. He walked over to Mr. Lyman and volunteered. I thought of that adagio couple long ago in Pacifica, and before I knew it, David was spinning me over his head in the legendary T-press.

It was a magnificent number, starting with women rippling across in front of their partners to curtsey as three gongs rang out. After turning back into closed position, we waltzed into a circle. The men left their partners and did cross canters to the center as the women went outward. The women then cantered in as the men spun out. Each girl went into a flat lift, a move where she wrapped her right arm under and around the man's left shoulder. David, with his right arm under the small of my back, spun me face up with my body parallel to the floor at waist level. He took my free hand and gently let me down to run around him.

We waltzed in more formations. From his right side I put my left arm around his shoulder and he spun me in a lift with my legs scissored in different directions. After coming down, we separated. When I turned back to face him, he laid my whole body across his shoulders, lifting to lock his arms with me over his head making the shape of a big T. Scary and disorienting as he spun, I had to stay as stiff as a board for it to work. It wasn't as easy as it looked.

Mr. Lyman had David and I posed for pictures in our Standard medley costume with another couple for advertising our Northern California Tour. They also put a huge blown up version of the picture in the hall of the Richards building. I couldn't believe it was actually me up there. (This picture is on the book cover.)

While changing into my practice outfit for class one day, the girls from the team began to question me. "How much do you like him?"

"Has he kissed you yet?" inquired my close friend, Sandy.

I often wondered why David had asked me out instead of Sandy. She would make an ideal companion with all the sweetness and curves most boys were looking for.

"No, he hasn't kissed me," I replied.

Sandy continued, "Well, maybe he's keeping it cool because you are partners and he doesn't want to ruin what you have right now."

"Ruin what we have?"

"Well, if it didn't work out and you wanted to stop seeing each other, it would be pretty uncomfortable since you would still have to be dance partners."

"That's true. He seems to be handling this the smart way.

Alexis and Dave Duke at the
Homecoming Spectacular.

Chapter 8

You Make Me Happy

The dancing and dating continued. One night before a competition, I found a note from David in one of my school books which read:

Princess Alexis,
　　The Prince counts each dreadful, long moment in eager anticipation to hold you in his arms and flow across the floor, as on angel wings, to the romantic sound of an ethereal slow waltz. With you tonight, the Prince will truly feel like the king of the ball.

Pretty corny, but I ate it up. There were times when we achieved placement in the top five or so at the competitions, but winning first or second continued to be elusive.

Our time together was full of rich activities, including going to many different places to eat. We took a scenic drive up Provo Canyon and also visited Salt Lake City's historic sites. We enjoyed several concerts as well. And all this time David never tried to kiss me. I held back because I felt he would prefer to make the first move.

Then one Monday morning after practice he handed me a large white envelope. "I wrote this for you," he said. "Read it when you get a minute by yourself."

When I was alone, I hurriedly opened it and was surprised to find an overwhelming seven-page letter expressing his feelings for me.

Dear Alexis,

Tonight I have some time and I feel relaxed, happy, grateful, and somewhat nostalgic. The intent of my words is not to write an English paper, but to write down the thoughts and feelings of my mind and heart as they have come to me in the past and as they are coming to me now. Thoughts and feelings are of little value unless there is someone who will truly listen and care. That is what a friend is. I'm grateful you are my friend.

You may ask why I am spending my time writing this when I can verbally talk to you. I guess the reason is that the written word has a lasting effect on both the writer and the reader. These words can be read many times for they are somewhat lasting, and perhaps you may do just that in the future. Perhaps these written symbols will add a different but ever so important facet to my desires to truly communicate to you as my friend. And then again, perhaps this is out of place, but you are to be the judge on that. I am only doing what I want to do. You must try to understand. If you find some of this offensive, have understanding. If you enjoy some of this, get as much joy from it as you possibly can, for that is the intent of my writing. Truly you deserve to have much joy in your life.

My mind reflects back about one year ago when we danced in the same Silver class. My first memory of you was when we were nominating girls to be in the Homecoming Queen pageant. As you left the room for us to vote, I asked a couple of people just what your name was so I could associate your face and name. I recognized your marvelous beauty then and told the class members to vote for you. As you can see, the class did not listen to me, but then how can average people recognize true beauty? They often cannot.

I next go to the east end of room 134 of the P.E. building one lovely fall day. We were all in a circle trying to learn the tango. That is the first time I remember dancing with you. You told me your name. On the next time around I remembered it, because your name interested me. I can recall the very spot on the dance floor where I said, "You are Alexis, aren't you?"

So dancing continued slowly and that was that. However, I remember we danced together one day when we were JVs learning the Sexton routine. Can you remember the 1,2,3, hop, kick, slide job we tried so hard to learn? We were also taught a waltz section where we traded partners. Even though it was just a one-day practice and no big deal, I did not like trading and getting another partner. I'm even worse today. I'm a one-partner man.

Life and school went on and even though I saw that you were different, I was tied up elsewhere not only in dancing, but in other areas of my life. As I look back, I can see how wise being tied up really was, because neither of us could dance. Perhaps if we were partners right off, we might have become frustrated.

"Who shall I take to the Arts Ball? Who is beautiful enough to be David Beckstead's date? Who would go with David Beckstead?" Very important questions that needed to be answered. After ten days of wanting to ask you and chickening out because I didn't want to make a mistake, I finally did it.

"Will you please go with me to the Arts Ball?" A very simple, sincere question that I'm glad was answered "yes." The Arts Ball—a classy, lovely event—was a very fitting and symbolic first date.

One Monday, five days before the Ball, we were all together at the west end of room 134 listening to one of Mr. Lyman's speeches and making arrangements for the dance team to perform in Orem the night of the ball. Perhaps fate, or someone else, had my partner Kathy home for the weekend. You asked me to dance a solo with you. Because of my dancing with Kathy, I was glad you made a move to do that solo, because I probably would not have. The next day I remembered going with you in the evening to practice—such a humble, but possibly directed, beginning of a marvelous dancing experience that has given me much pleasure and happiness in the past and will continue to grow until we can dance for the angels.

How can I tell you how much I appreciated you as my partner? As I would take you in my arms, dancing seemed to come alive. You were so pleasant to be around. And, as I have said before, you made me happy. We seemed to fit together nicely and I loved to hold you.

Well, our solo was scary but afterward, the Ball was fun. I felt like I was a king back in the good old days dancing the Viennese waltz with the queen. You impressed me as being a lady, someone worth rising to be a gentleman for. Ever since then, you have helped me to rise above the average and be a gentleman by your always acting like a lady. I remember at first calling you "conservative" for lack of a better word, to describe you for what I now call "a lady." I'm so glad for your "conservatism." You helped me rise.

Friday, March 31, 1978, was the International Ball. I gave you a ride. We danced a time or two. After one particular quickstep, you told me I was a very smooth dancer. I drove you home. It was the day before your birthday, and you invited me in for a piece of your birthday cake. The cake was good, but I remember very well talking to you that night and how you listened to me share all my far-out ideas. For some reason, I felt at ease talking to you about the feelings of my heart.

Remember how we decided the best way to run the dance team was with love? We said that love could conquer all and that internal motivation was the only way. We said that this year we would be examples of love. It is this year now. Are we being examples of love? That is a question we should not only ask ourselves today but for the rest of our lives.

Alexis, I believe in love, and I believe that it is the motivating force behind every good thing. God is God because he loves. Above all else, I hope throughout our lives we can love everyone without compulsion, expecting nothing in return. If we do this, we will receive everything in return and the pearl of great price will be ours. Communion with the Spirit and God will be ours.

After a show or two, summer came and we went home. I intended to write you. But, of course, I had to wait awhile so I didn't make it look obvious. Then your picture arrived, which gave me the great opportunity to call you up. As you know, the picture is nice, and I made a frame for it from wood I took off the old barn. Today I see it several times each day because it sits on my desk.

"May I speak to Alexis please?" I looked forward every few weeks to saying that. I enjoyed very much talking to you on the phone, and I loved to share in your summer and also have you share in mine.

It is now August 29th and I'm leaning against my car when I see you again after a long summer. I stayed that evening for dinner, which was very good. I felt happy again and looked forward to being with you this semester, both dancing and dating.

Dating you presented me with a problem and still does at times. That problem is this: *How can I date her, and dance with her, and be her friend without causing her any hassles in her life?* That has caused me a lot of worry and I hope I'm behaving well. I also might say that I would appreciate your honest opinions about these three areas of our lives whenever it is convenient. Be honest with me and I'll be honest with you. Let our friendship be built upon lasting experiences or let our departure be one of peace and understanding. It is often hard to act like mature adults when feelings are involved, but this gives us an opportunity to rise above the world and build a special relationship. That may sound weird, but I'm a dreamer.

So here it is mid-semester. We have done some fun things, gone some fun places, and danced a lot. I think it has been great, and you have been a wonderful friend and have made me happy.

Yesterday I stopped by to see you out of the clear blue because I felt good and wanted to know what you had done during the day. You were not expecting me, and you didn't have your hair curled or any makeup on. I got the feeling that you were not too pleased to have me around just then. I said you looked wonderful, but you didn't believe me and I didn't like that.

Alexis, has it ever occurred to you that it isn't your curled hair that I enjoy. It is your hair that I enjoy. It isn't your makeup that I enjoy. It is your naturally beautiful face that I enjoy. It isn't your hair or your face that I enjoy, but it is your soul that I enjoy. It isn't your soul that I enjoy, but I enjoy your intelligence. (May I say that I truly appreciate your efforts to look nice all the time, but I hope you can see that I like 'you' and my compliments are for "you," not your hairspray.) You are beautiful from the inside out, not the outside in.

Speaking of your intelligence (that is the part of you which interests me right now), I want to get to know you, the endless you.

Alexis, I often tell you that you make me happy. Dancing with you is one of the most heavenly things I've done on this earth. I'm so grateful that you put up with me. I could go on, but I think that by now you will understand if I simply say that you are the greatest.

It is getting late. My eyes hurt very much, my fingers can hardly write, and my body is tired. But my heart is happy, and I am glad that I've spent the time to write this letter to you. I hope you'll enjoy it. I look forward someday, Alexis, to putting my arms around you and then warm body to warm body, soul to soul, intelligence to intelligence, to not verbally say thanks, but to let our intelligences intermingle with each other and relate to each other thoughts, words, and ideas that you and I cannot understand, but can feel with every particle of our being. Then we will begin to understand the meaning of such phrases as: "thank you," "you make me happy," "I love you."

If you have found some of my words too personal, please don't worry. I'll do what you want and I'll understand. There is much time ahead and I want no pressures on either of us, only to dance and enjoy each other's friendship. Now read this again and try to understand what I have tried to say. You make me happy and I think you are the greatest.

With love from your dance partner

Wow! I was bowled over. At last, I finally knew what he really thought, his reminiscing showing what stood out for him. His many compliments made me light-headed.

What a mind the boy had! I had never met or dated any person who thought so deeply and sensitively about things the way he did. It was like a breath of fresh air. He made my mind expand and stretch itself. I was happy he enjoyed dancing with me as much as I did with him. Yet, again, there was part of me that kept holding back. Maybe I had watched too many old romantic movies, but I kept expecting the ceiling to fall in, or something similar, and it hadn't yet. But this letter made me want to take a step closer to him, continue our friendship, and spend time together. I just hoped that he didn't ask for a commitment. I still wanted time to dance, time to live.

That evening after studying at the library, David took me for a drive up the mountain where the Provo Temple stood—a beautiful church building lit up from top to bottom. In our religion we believe that marriage can go on forever. We also believe in saving ourselves for the one person we make a commitment to for eternity, giving ourselves totally only after marriage. David and I had that understanding. The courtship thing to us was not for here and now. It was to find a partner for the long-haul. A church temple was where we could make that kind of eternal promise.

He stopped the car on the hill near the temple where it overlooked the valley below. It was a glorious sight. We talked for a while about what we did that day and discussed some of the subjects we studied.

Then I brought up the topic he most wanted to hear. "I read your letter. It must have taken quite awhile to write. I appreciated hearing how you felt about everything we had done. There's just one question."

"What's that?"

"May I hug you?"

He smiled. "Yes."

We put our arms around each other, and I found myself in perfect, delectable contentment, not wanting to let go. It was where I belonged—safe, secure, and so right.

After gazing at the city lights a while longer, he drove me to my apartment. He enfolded me in his arms again at my door, then left.

Chapter 9

Touring Magic

Our charter bus stopped at a station in the dark. The driver exited, and a new driver climbed aboard. After observing the passengers, the new driver commented, "Well, aren't we all cozy and comfy?"

It was true. In every seat couples were using each other as pillows, trying to sleep during the late ride. David's broad chest was very comfortable, especially with his arm wrapped around me.

"We will be in Fallon, Nevada, in a couple of hours," announced the driver.

We were on our way to tour Northern California, a well-earned opportunity to share our talents with others. The troupe included the Brigham Young University Latin, Standard, and Social Dance teams. The difference between the teams was the style used. The Social Team danced American style. The Standard and Latin teams used International Style. American rhythms are similar, but in Standard dancing the positioning allows the couple to break away from one another.

The next evening at the Fallon High School gym, we performed our adagio number for the first time in public, and the thrill of it felt like a fairy tale. I recalled the dancers I saw many years ago in Pacifica. Here I was in their place, representing the same university. "Dad, you were right. I *could* do it!"

As we continued our tour, the more I appeared in front of audiences, the more relaxed and confident I grew.

One of my favorite numbers we did was a Viennese waltz choreographed by Vernon Brock. Starting in a diagonal line one couple waltzed down the center as we each spun outward making way. We changed the direction of the diagonal, then, formed an X, which turned. The men picked up twirling partners. After moving to a circle we did step-brush-hops, open right turns, and then blockbusters where each man lifted his partner to do a scissor kick on a big climax in the song. The music was so enchanting and the moves so delightful that I put my heart and soul into it each time.

At our performance in Hayward, a town in the San Francisco Bay area, someone handed me a note from my former boss whom I had worked for the previous summer. His message said he was attending the program with a couple of my secretary friends, and they wanted to meet me afterward.

Curiously, after the last number, David took my hand and said, "Come with me," walking me to a secluded corner back stage. I thought he wanted to have a private conversation. But, instead, he backed me into the wall and kissed me passionately. He was like a volcano whose top finally came off, letting loose all its power.

When our lips parted, I looked at him in surprise and smiled. "Couldn't take it anymore, huh?"

"Nope."

I put my arms around him and returned the favor just as intensely. The indulgence left me limp.

"Why did you wait so long, David?"

"I wanted to be friends and get to know you first before I tried anything physical."

I was impressed with his restraint but glad he had succumbed to his desires.

Reluctantly, I reminded him that I had friends waiting to see me. With my cheeks flushed, I pulled him out to the hall where my boss greeted me with, "Whoever would have thought my secretary could dance like that? It was beautiful!"

"Thank you. I am so glad you could come. This is my dance partner, David."

They nodded hello and I introduced everyone. It was nice to see my friends again. I think my old employer now understood why I turned down the permanent job he had offered me the last summer. How could I miss out on college and dancing like this?

Our next performance was closer to Pacifica, and my parents planned to attend. Before the show, I watched the entrance anxiously for them. They told me in an earlier communication that they were very excited to see me dance.

It was not always like that. My mind went back to when I was a teenager. Our church had two youth dances a month with live bands. One evening Dad said to me, "I know why you like to go to those dances. You want to bear hug with all those boys."

Teasingly I replied, "Dad, just let me show you how I dance." Then I walked up to him and put my hands on his shoulders. "I always keep my arms between me and the boy. Anytime he tries to squeeze me too tight, I do this." I shoved my dad backwards comically several times. "Those boys don't have a chance to get fresh with me," I joked. Then I shoved him again. "Do you see what I mean?" He laughed and replied that he didn't worry about me any longer.

My father was always protective. Although he may have had concerns when I was younger, now he encouraged me in my desire to perfect this gorgeous art form.

I giggled to myself when another memory came to me. I visualized the first time I ever saw my father fast dance like the teens of the 70's. I thought he was strictly a waltz and foxtrot man. But after I finished slow dancing with my dad at a church ball, a voice from the band rang out, "Jeremiah was a Bullfrog! Was a good friend of mine!" To my surprise my father started gyrating around the floor to the popular song, "Joy to the World." I stopped dancing to laugh at the hysterical scene.

He grinned at me. "What's the matter, didn't you know that your old daddy could Rock and Roll?" It wasn't anything like my friends' moves, but a jerking of his own interpretation. I had to hold my stomach.

Suddenly I was pulled out of my reverie as my Mom, Dad, my little brother, and sister came through the door. I ran to my dad in full costume and threw my arms around him. "What is this?" he exclaimed, looking at me in surprise. "I didn't recognize you. I thought I was being attacked by a strange woman."

Having been away from my family for three months, it was so nice to be with them again. They commented on my costume and quickly found a seat. During the program I tried to dance my best. My family was in awe as they watched David spin me over his head in our adagio number.

When I introduced them to David after the show, my little brother, Matt, said, "You're strong!"

"He sure is," agreed my mother.

My director allowed me to go home with my family that night. I treasured our time together. We were very close. My parents seemed proud of me, and it gave me great satisfaction to make them happy.

The following day my parents drove me to our Oakland show, but the performance had a hitch. As I was spinning around in the T-press during our lift routine, I heard a loud "kaboom!" then heard a gasp from the audience.

When I came down from my dizzy movement, I noticed one of the girls shaking like a leaf as she went into her ending pose. Off stage I exclaimed, "What happened?"

"I dropped Mona in the T-press," said her partner.

It was probably a seven-foot drop. We all surrounded Mona, asking if she was okay. "That hurt so bad," she moaned, rubbing her side. "But I'll be fine."

Her partner couldn't stop saying he was sorry as Mona continued to grimace. I appreciated that David never lost control when I was in that position and felt real gratitude for the farm that had given him his astonishing musculature. Luckily, we had no more mishaps as we continued north.

Our California tour had provided the extraordinary opportunity to share our gifts with others, giving us greater experience in the world of performance. In the process, the dream of a thirteen-year-old girl came true.

After our final show in Eureka, I stayed overnight at the home of a couple that had met one another at BYU. They had two adorable children, a gorgeous home, and seemed so content. I wondered if my own story would have such a happy ending.

David lifting Alexis in the T-press

Chapter 10

The Test

During Christmas break, David drove out to Pacifica to meet my parents. They let me know in a hurry that they approved of him, but I responded with ambivalence. I dreamed of a powerful confirmation deep in my soul that said, "Yes, this is the man." But it hadn't come. Thankfully, David was content to keep the status quo. I wanted my options left open in case the affirmation did not appear.

The winter semester continued like the fall with classes, homework, dancing, and spending all my free time with a farm boy.

Soon it was time for the girls' choice dance, "Preference." Of course, I asked David to go with me. After all, he was my preferred man. At the dance we knew moves to every song. Making our way around the floor, people stared as if we were Fred Astaire and Ginger Rogers. But we felt like angels with wings, dancing for the gods.

Rehearsals with David continued hour after hour, day after day. Dance music that stirred the soul was always playing in Room 134 on campus. Curious passersby often peeked through the doors, catching their breath as they watched the swirling couples move counterclockwise. It was quite a sight. We continued to improve our individual routines for competition.

One foxtrot song we rehearsed to became our favorite, entitled *Dance in the Old-Fashioned Way*, written by Charles Aznavour. It talked about reaching highs as we moved around the floor.

In March of 1979 Mr. Lyman informed us that the NCAA Basketball Tournament was to be held at Brigham Young University's Marriot Center, and we had been asked to be the half-time entertainment for the final Western Division game between DePaul and UCLA. Mr. Lyman wanted the Standard team to do the España number with our capes and shawls. We were ecstatic at the opportunity.

When the day of the game arrived, we waited nervously in a back room of the Marriot

Center. We had jitters, not only because of the audience size, but because this contest was being televised, and clips of our performance might be aired.

UCLA took the lead in the first part of the game. When the halftime buzzer rang, the sweaty UCLA team members ran past us on their way out. We were overwhelmed by their size—like giants from some science fiction movie. It seemed like our heads only came up to their belly buttons.

My heart jumped when the broadcaster announced us. As we entered the gigantic arena filled with thousands of fans, I was shaking. The dramatic Spanish rhythm sounded, and we began our exhibition. We hadn't danced half of the number, before the UCLA players suddenly decided they wanted to practice early. They ran out dribbling, shooting baskets, and yelled for us to get out of their way. When seven-foot goliaths start intimidating you, you don't stick around. Some of the UCLA supporters on the sidelines joined in, hollering for us to get lost. Looking at each other disconcertedly, we exited as quickly as possible. Many of the girls were in tears. The rest of us were just plain mad.

We changed quickly and joined the audience. What happened next, no one suspected. The Utah fans, livid at UCLA's rudeness and self-importance, booed UCLA and cheered mightily for DePaul throughout the next half of the game. With this encouragement, DePaul took the lead and won the game 95 to 91, becoming kings of the Western Region Conference. After the embarrassment we had undergone, we were overjoyed at the outcome.

At our spring ballroom concert we performed all the numbers we had learned that year for an audience who appreciated us, making it a totally different experience than the previous one.

The next Friday I gave David a hand-written invitation to see an old movie with me on campus. He agreed to go on Saturday. After studying in the library that evening, he drove me home, and kissed me hungrily at my apartment door. After a big sigh, he blurted out, "Maybe we should start thinking about getting married."

I backed away quickly. "David, I don't think I'm ready to get married yet."

He was hurt. "Don't you want to at least think about it?"

"I have thought about it. If you want me to get married, then I think we better cool it off. We'd better stop seeing each other."

"I thought you cared about me," he said incredulously.

"I do, but I don't want to get married."

I had injured him. He tried many other arguments, but they were all met with my desire to end the relationship. Walking away with his hands in his pockets and his head down, he kicked a rock before disappearing into the dark.

Talk about pain. I was learning it firsthand. I never knew I could cause so much misery and be so miserable doing it. My problem? I was still waiting for the big hammer over the head that said, "This is it!"

I liked being with David, but I thought I was supposed to feel more than I did when the right guy came along. My trouble may have been watching too many old movies. But eternity is a long time. Not wanting to make any commitment until I knew with absolute certainty I was doing the right thing, it didn't seem fair to continue dating, giving him false hope.

The next day, Saturday, I moped around the apartment and did some studying, eventually deciding to go to that old film I wanted to see. As I walked to the building on campus alone feeling depressed, through the glass door I saw David sitting on the floor in the foyer looking like he was waiting for me. I wanted to turn and run. Instead,

I did the next best thing and walked past him into the Ladies Room, hoping he would disappear. When I came out, he was leaning against a wall watching for me. Stepping to me, he suggested, "Since we are both here, we might as well watch the show together."

"Alright," I agreed. We walked into the auditorium in silence and sat down. *The Unsinkable Molly Brown*, started and we did not say anything until we left the theater.

"You might as well let me give you a ride home," he said. "We need to talk."

"David, there is nothing to talk about. You want a more lasting relationship and I'm not ready. That's all there is to it."

As we walked to his car and traveled home, he tried every way possible to convince me that we were right for each other, but I would not listen. He left my apartment looking totally disheartened. I hated myself for making him feel sad.

Monday was awkward. Here we were "not seeing each other" and yet David and I had to dance many hours together each day because of our obligations. It was terribly uncomfortable for both of us. After the morning practice I charged up the 106 stairs to campus and headed for work. I went directly to Marge, my boss, an older lady with glasses and grey hair swept up into a bun. She was like my mother away from home, a special friend. I had kept Marge informed of my love life.

We had a tradition in the office—whenever one of the secretaries kissed a boy for the first time, she had to buy ice cream for the other secretaries. I bought ice cream for the girls and Marge when David gave me my first kiss.

"Marge," I exclaimed, "It is so awful! David wants to get married, and I don't want to because I think I should feel more for him. We aren't going to date anymore, but I have to dance with him four hours a day. It is so hard."

Concern and compassion filled her face. "Well, maybe this separation will be good for you. After being with him less, maybe you will discover that you really do love him, or you may find the opposite. You may find you are perfectly content to go on without him. Look at it as a positive thing that can help you make up your mind."

"Oh, Marge, thank you." I threw my arms around her. "That makes me feel so much better. I think you are right. This may be a kind of test." She smiled, and we both went to work typing papers. It was wonderful to have such a motherly friend so far from home.

Over the next week I discovered how wise Marge was. I began to feel the void of David's absence. He no longer walked me to class, and I endured my evenings alone. Because of our closeness and spending so much time together, I hated not being with him. During team rehearsal the next Friday, David had us run through my favorite foxtrot section in our medley. As I rested my arm on his muscle and smelled his cologne, a wave of incredible attraction swept over me. Taking my right hand in his, we lowered and stepped out moving as one. The thought of never dancing in his arms or talking with him again cut me to the heart.

After class when he changed his shoes, I sat down next to him. "David, can we keep seeing each other, but not talk about marriage for awhile? I just want to be with you."

He smiled. "Sure we can. I want to be with you, too."

I heaved a sigh of relief. We went on as if nothing happened and spent as much time with each other as before. It was nice not feeling pressured. He joked about almost naming me 326, the file number that came after his old flame 325.

A couple of weeks passed by, and one day while typing papers at work, I recounted David's amazing qualities. It dawned on me that he would make a great father and teach his children to work hard. I had lost my desire to date anyone else and turned down other boys all the time. David was the only one I wanted to be around. The thought of him not being part of my life seemed too terrible to comprehend.

I guess I do love him, I said to myself. *I do want to marry him.* When I mentally formed the words, a beautiful peace surrounded me, and the assurance I wanted sunk deep into my heart.

So this is what it is like, I surmised. No nuclear explosions, loud gongs, or rockets shooting off — just peace. For me love came as quiet and restful as the rising sun in a turquoise sky, slow and subtle, but beautiful and full of light. It was like the perfect foxtrot gliding effortlessly through space.

That night in the library at our usual meeting place in a secluded corner, I came up behind my man, put my arms around him, and said, "I love you," for the first time.

"What brought this on?" he questioned as he turned to face me.

"Oh, I've been thinking a lot about you and me, and I decided you are the person I want to spend the rest of my life with," I answered.

His face lit up with the good news. Walking me behind a bookcase, his kisses were filled with longing and desire. We left the library and he drove me home with the song "Laura" playing. The romantic strains set the stage perfectly for a discussion of our future. He repeated his dream of returning to Preston to set up his practice and build a big beautiful home. He wanted at least six children, maybe eight. He said that he would have plenty of money to buy some land and maybe have horses.

I started to sob.

"Why are you crying?" he asked.

"I just never thought I would be so lucky."

He pulled me closer to him. As I continued to weep, he whispered softly, "I always wanted a woman to cry on my shoulder."

Chapter 11

Blackpool and Beyond

In May of 1979 the thirty-two members of the Brigham Young University Ballroom Dance Team, dressed in navy blue suit coats with the college insignia on their pockets, walked into the ballroom at Blackpool, England. Our eyes went upward as we turned to examine the double gothic balconies surrounding the floor, which was the size of two basketball courts. A large stage with a band was just off the center. As I watched the German team practice their medley, I said to myself, *We certainly don't look that refined.*

The Germans left the area and the Japanese team ran through their dance. The number was elegant, clean, and their posture beyond comparison. They were even better than the

Germans. We took our turn and left feeling we needed more practice.

Lining up to compete that evening, I was scared to death. This was the most famous competition in the world. All great dancers seek a title at the British Ballroom Dance Championships. We did not even dream of competing as individuals, for it would take many years and professional coaching to refine our skills to that point. But we did have great hopes for our team medley.

Later that evening at the ballroom crowded with spectators, we began our exhibition. A band played our song from sheet music. It sounded quite a bit different from the recording we were used to, making it a challenge for us. In the end, the Japanese team won first place. The Germans took second, and BYU was third in the Standard category.

Our Latin team fared better by taking second. Wayne Cluff, of that team, said to us when it was all over, "Well, that was the best we could do. I can honestly say we have never done it better."

Knowing we had not held back was a good feeling for all of us.

The experience of just being at Blackpool filled me with wonder as I watched the huge arena swirl with colorful, dramatic movement during the individual competitions. Even after all the hours I had spent on dancing, I still felt like a beginner compared to those competing. A person would have to sacrifice a great deal to achieve that perfection. I loved dancing. It made me happy. But I was not willing to give up all the other things that were important to me to be that good—other things such as a family.

Our company put on shows in concert halls as we traveled across England. We performed our Viennese waltz, Standard medley, our Blackpool competition number, "España" with shawls and capes, and our three-couple adagio number. The Latin team had their own set of numbers and a few solos. (David and I had given up doing a solo because of limited time before we left for the tour.) I never tired of repeating the show. Performing was what it was all about to me—dancing for the sheer joy of it.

We stayed overnight in the homes of host families and were able to do a little sightseeing, always doubling with Sandy and Wayne on our excursions. They were dear friends. It was exciting to explore London together. In front of Big Ben Sandy and I asked a policeman, or bobby, if we could have our picture with him.

In a thick British brogue he questioned, "What is this? 'Charlie's Angels?'"

We laughed at our comparison to hot TV, undercover policewomen.

When I was assigned to room with Sandy, I confided about my relationship with my farmer. David and I hadn't made our engagement official to the others yet, but I had to tell someone.

After England we boarded a boat and crossed the Channel. We performed in France, Belgium, and Holland and did more sight seeing. It was wonderful to share it all with the man I loved.

One day when we toured the ruins of an old castle, David pulled me back to lag behind our group. In a far corner, his lips melded into mine. There I was, with my prince in a castle. What could be more corny or romantic? Yes, life was just like a fairy tale.

That August David and I were married in the Logan Temple, thirty miles south of his parents' farm. We used the picture of our first date for the newspaper announcement while the wedding invitations showed us in costume, posed in a throw-away oversway—an arching lung line in closed dance position.

It was a beautiful wedding. We were married for eternity. Partway through our reception we performed eight dance routines for our friends and family. A band was provided for general dancing with hundreds of people attending. Sandy drove up from Provo to give us her good wishes, bringing a fiancé with her who seemed like a great guy. Sandy was the kind of friend I planned on staying in touch with my whole life.

My father surprised me by reciting a poem he wrote. Dad had often recited poetry as I was growing up, so this was not unlike him. He was a sentimentalist and I loved him for it.

An Ode To …

Laughter . . . ripples across the summit of my years
Jiggling days with delightful reverberations,
Sets askance would-be mundane seasons,
Alexis is . . .

Poignant moment... bright face and delightsome smile
Disturbs the heartbeat for awhile.
(From placid pond to surging mountain stream)
Much at home a water sprite
Poised above cascading falls
Which echo twixt old granite walls
Makes time pause in weightless flight,
Then clefts the emerald pool
And water music bubbles back to my waiting ear.

Sierra meadow . . . splashed in color of brilliant hue,
Basking 'neath iridescent light
Wears a cap of azure blue,
And tassel of fowl in autumn flight.
Who lies mid wild flowers there
And wields the brush of mirth on nature's canvas?
Alexis is…

Seasons change . . . memories reel through this grey head
And strum about the shadows of another day;
Weaving a tableau of feet a tread on crystal floor,
And through capacious halls they play.
Lithe figure pirouettes with captivating grace
No child this with platinum curls and
Questioning infant face.

Now, born up a woman; eagerly clasps unto her breast
A refreshing draught from the fountain head.[1]
Alexis is . . .

"Thank you, Dad," I said gratefully as I hugged him. He was an ideal father to his six children, spending a lot of time with us over the years. I recalled the beautiful mountain meadow we discovered while hiking together one summer and our annual trek to Kaweah River in the Sierra Mountains that had waterfalls and pools we played in.

---

1   fountain head = Christ

While I was growing up, Dad often drove us to Golden Gate Park for bike riding, and to the beach for hot dog roasts and kickball. He took us swimming and roller skating and taught us to play baseball and croquet.

After I kissed his cheek, I said, "You're the best father in the whole world," and I meant it.

David and I honeymooned at my family cabin in the California Sierras. There wasn't a soul around for miles. Then we hiked to Kaweah River, my favorite family wonderland. We walked down a steep hill to the river then climbed up the side of a fifty-foot waterfall. Above the falls we rock hopped another mile to our special spot where we dove off waterfalls and swam in the warm sun.

David's commentary was, "This is worse than the movies." It was a romantic honeymoon, but dancing had made it the perfect courtship.

Alexis with her father at her wedding reception

David and Alexis dancing at their wedding reception

Chapter 12

Glory Days

As seniors, David and I were enlisted to instruct two beginning Bronze classes. At that time married couples could not be on the dance team, but we could compete. Our biggest goal was to win first place at the International Ball. To help us achieve it, we set up a plan to rehearse two hours each morning and take private lessons from local professionals. Markedly we increased our skill in how to lower and extended the size of our steps. Our objective came closer when we won first place in a slow waltz competition at Mr. Lyman's private ballroom in American Fork.

Meanwhile, we joined an advanced Latin dance class with the further ambition to obtain our Gold Latin medal. Having watched the social dance team on our California tour, we decided to round out our skills by participating in social classes as well.

I will never forget the joy of reaching such a height in our ballroom ability. At the school dances, we stole the show, moving to anything and everything they played.

One night we requested the lively swing, "In the Mood," by Glen Miller. As the band wailed out the tune, David and I burned up the rug! It was (to use an expression of the 70s) "far out!"

Sue Jensen, my first dance teacher, moved back to Utah around this time and I looked her up. It was a happy reunion. Her daughter, Alexis, had grown a great deal. She was born when I was a teenager. Sue explained at that time, "I gave her your name, because I wanted to have a girl just like you." Deeply moved, I hoped I could measure up to Sue's expectations.

Upon asking Sue if I could borrow her ballroom dress, she told me to keep it. She never planned on using it again.

I wore the yellow chiffon gown for the International Ball, which came in November. Entering the campus ballroom with my handsome escort, I was overcome with *déjà vu*. The music and swirling couples reincarnated my first dance lab. I could hear the echo of my own words, "THIS IS WHAT I WANT TO DO! I WANT TO

BE A GREAT DANCER!" As a freshman I had felt like a foreigner, but now I was in my territory and the floor seemed to call to me.

By the time the competition was through, we won three of the five Standard dances, taking first place in the highest category. After years of hard work, we were very happy. It was like making it to the top of Mount Everest.

I must confess my conflicting feelings at this time, however. Although we met our goal, I never found complete satisfaction in competing. We all knew they were very subjective, depending on who judged that night or when they happened to glance your way, with each judge having a different opinion on what aspects of the presentation were most important. Even though we lucked out with the judges that night, in the back of our minds we felt Randy, our team president, and his partner Mona were the best. Admittedly, though, the competition had motivated us to improve ourselves.

The opportunity to instruct beginners was a growing experience as we passed on the technique we knew. One day in class David taught our students a sequence of steps and asked the group to repeat it. He leaned over to me and whispered, "Did we look this bad when we first started?"

"I think we did," I said quietly.

As we taught throughout the semester, several pupils with limited abilities became a model for understanding. Although they had no natural talent, their eagerness led them to practice longer and harder than the rest, always asking for help. No matter how difficult it was for them to catch on, they would not give up. After three months, we saw amazing progress in these individuals. At first we did not have much hope that our students with two left feet would ever look good, but here they were getting the hang of it and were actually a pleasure to watch. It was a lesson in hard work and tenacity overcoming limitations.

We were pleased with the efforts of the whole class. Near the end of the semester at one of the Wednesday night dance competitions, several of our students came up to David and said, "We want to compete against the Gold couples using our Bronze routines. Is that okay?"

David looked at me, then back at them, replying, "Go ahead. What can it hurt? It will be good for you."

A short time later, Wayne Cluff, came over to talk to us. "Do you realize that your beginners are beating some of the Gold couples? That's incredible."

"We can't believe it either."

"You guys are doing a great job" Wayne exclaimed.

"Thanks," we answered. But we knew our pupils' success was the result of their application.

Graduation came with mixed feelings. During our time at Brigham Young we made some wonderful friends. Leaving them would be sad, but the memories we made would be engraved upon our hearts forever. The knowledge we gained would travel with us. We looked forward to the future with excitement with a hopeful eye.

Alexis and David competing at Mr. Lyman's
private ballroom in American Fork

Chapter 13

Losing the Best

After we graduated from college David accepted a spot at Creighton University Medical School in Omaha, Nebraska. Our second year in Omaha, my church leaders asked me to be the assistant youth dance director over the Dance Festival. The director and I asked each of the seven youth groups in the area to come up with their own dance. I found myself in a high school gym filled with teenagers.

Leaning toward a microphone, I said, "Welcome to our dress rehearsal. I am Alexis Beckstead. First we will run through each dance, and then I will show you the finale, which is very easy.

After the groups did their dance numbers— waltz, Charleston, swing, and polka, etc.—

practicing entrances and exits, David and I performed a Viennese waltz solo. The teenager's eyes were riveted on us. Oh, it was so good to be in the arms of my man again. The music was classical, cheery and lighthearted making the routine feel like a big romp. Several times David lifted me in his strong arms and twirled me in the air. When the song ended, the kids cheered. They paid closer attention to my instructions after that.

I thought about Sue Jensen, and what she had done for me. Here I was in her shoes putting on a Dance Festival in Omaha, Nebraska, passing on the legacy. It was fitting that it took place in Fred Astaire's hometown.

After the arrival of two children and David's graduation from medical school, we moved to Phoenix, Arizona for his residency in Family Practice Medicine. One Saturday evening in January, I went to answer the phone.

"Is that you, Alexis?" It was my mother's voice. "Is David there with you?"

"Yes, what is it Mom?" She was silent for a moment.

"Your father has been killed in a car accident tonight," she said in the saddest voice I had ever heard from her.

"Oh, Mom!" She let me cry for a while before continuing. Dad was only sixty-three and Mom was fifty-six. She would be without him for a long time. It must have been hard for her to make the six phone calls to her children to explain the news.

Finally she gave the details. "He had been flying with a buddy. When they were done, your dad dropped his friend off and continued driving home. Going around a horseshoe bend, he passed over the line and hit another car head on. He was killed instantly and so was the other driver. We think your father was distracted in some way."

My mother said she would call back again to let me know about the funeral. She expressed her love for me and her thankfulness for the gospel of Jesus Christ.

I had never lost anyone that close to me before. Because of the suddenness, it was like being kicked in the stomach by a mule. I was overwhelmed with loss. Although I cried for days, somehow the Lord comforted me in the knowledge that we would be together again. But still I mourned that I would not hear that loving voice, or see the tenderness in his baby blue eyes when he looked at me. My children would never know my father like I knew him. The pain was acute. But even in my suffering, I felt the love of God. A love that said, "I've taken him unto myself. His work is finished. He was a faithful servant."

David was gone a lot with his residency work during this time. When he finally came home Monday night, I asked him to watch our children so I could have some quiet time alone. In my room I listened to a cassette tape my father had recorded for me only a month or two before, which was now a priceless treasure. There was one section I especially wanted to hear again:

> During World War II the high during pilot training was soloing. You can imagine the thrill and excitement building as each one of us got close to the point where we were going to solo. There was a high *espirit de corp* among the group, and the feeling was, "Who soloed today? Who made it today?" I often think how, beyond the veil, as we have interactions and socialize, we might ask each other, "Who's coming today? Who made it today?" with a real excitement. The thing that is edifying is the hope that we can all be together again someday. We can share and do things together. Just think of all the fun we had while you were kids in this life. And if that's so, what a wonderful hope.

As I listened, I remembered that Dad's parents and brother had preceded him in death. They were probably very happy to see him again. My father's own words gave me much solace in a difficult time.

The last thing Dad said to me on the tape was, "In all your comings and goings, love. It's the only thing worthwhile." It was something I would never forget and would come to believe myself.

The eulogy, given by my Dad's flying partner, Skip, made us laugh as he spoke about the fun life my father led. Skip also quoted some silly limericks Dad had written in letters.

My mother had asked each of us to say a few words about Dad at the funeral. I enjoyed hearing my siblings revel in moments they treasured. When my turn came, I read the above quotes and the message that Dad sent me in college:

If you aren't brave enough, courageous enough, wise or adventurous enough to take advantage of the things that present themselves, then you just kind of exist in life; you don't really live. … Live, Honey. Dance to Live!

It was fitting that he died on the way home from flying, living life to the fullest. I think Dad would be proud of the "living" I was to do.

Alexis and her father Buzz at their
cabin in the mountains

PART II

Teaching Dance

When I was young, my heart would soar
Every time I danced 'cross the floor.
Now I share the fun
And teach everyone.
It is what I adore even more.

Alexis

Chapter 14

Is There a Need?

At a grocery store in Preston, Idaho, a woman in her sixties stopped me as I pushed a cart full of children. "Mrs. Beckstead, that doctor husband of yours is so wonderful and good to me. I told him that I made up my mind. When he dies, I'm going to die because I just can't live without him!"

I laughed.

"Are all these kids yours?" she asked. "How many children do you have now?"

"I have six—four boys and two girls."

"Oh, isn't that nice?" remarked the lady. "I like large families. Did your husband deliver them?"

"He delivered four of them," I replied.

"How special that must have been. Say, I remember you and your husband performed a beautiful waltz in town when you were engaged. Do you ever dance anymore?"

"I'm afraid not, Mrs. Merton. My husband is so busy with his family practice and me with the children that we don't have time anymore."

"Oh, that's a shame. You are beautiful dancers. I'd love to see you dance again, sometime. Goodbye Mrs. Beckstead."

That night at my dream home on Valley View Drive, I sat down to dinner with my family and spoke to David about the latest news. "I read they are now having the National Amateur Ballroom Dance Championships in the Marriot Center at BYU each year. I'd like to take the older children. They need to see the kind of dancing we did and know how beautiful it is."

"It would be good for them," he admitted. "Unfortunately, one of my patients is due to deliver a baby anytime and I better stick around."

That was fine with me, I had gotten used to David's hectic schedule as a doctor. I knew he was doing important things for the people in town, and I never felt resentment.

When the Championships came, I got a sitter for my younger children and drove the three hours to Provo. As I sat in the Marriot Center,

I reminisced on the evening I performed in the Homecoming Spectacular and those exhausting practices that led David to hold my hand for the first time. David and I had attended many concerts in that mammoth building during our college days. I chuckled at being chased off the court by the UCLA team and the satisfaction I felt at watching them lose. Then pride overflowed as I recalled my graduation ceremony held there.

As the lift competition began, I wondered if the adagio dances would keep my kids interest at the ages of eight, ten, twelve, and fourteen. But they were engrossed and on the edge of their seats the entire time.

I was surprised when high school teams came out to compete. One school danced a tremendous number to a medley of James Bond music. In the end, the girls shot the boys with their finger guns, and all the men fell down dead. The high school students also had individual competitions, and I was astounded at how good they were.

Later that night we saw the National Amateur Competition. The floor was a weaving flow of color with the women dressed in ornate, feathered gowns reminding me of exotic fans as they twirled. The expertise was superlative, bringing back a flood of Blackpool memories.

My children particularly liked a country swing specialty where one giant cowboy danced with three girls and threw them all over the place. He ended with one female on each hip and the third between his legs. The crowd gave their thunderous approval. I wish I could have stayed for the next day of competition.

That night as we drove home, the younger children fell asleep in their seats. But my oldest son Dave was awake next to me.

"Dave, I couldn't believe all the high school students competing. I didn't know ballroom had become so popular in the Utah schools."

"I'd like to dance like that."

"You would, Dave?"

"Sure, I wish we had a team at our high school in Preston," he said.

Dave soon fell asleep, and I began asking a host of questions in my mind. Why couldn't we have this in Idaho? Who could we get to direct a team in Preston? Neal Swann, who taught David, is gone a lot with his work. Other than him, David and I are the only ones in town who know how to do this kind of dancing. But David's too busy. Would he support me in teaching? He wouldn't want me to neglect the kids.

My thoughts became a prayer:

Dear Father in Heaven,

I have the idea of starting a high school ballroom team in Preston. Is it a good idea or am I just being unrealistic? If you want me to do this, please let everything come together and work out. Help me feel enthusiasm, and let David be supportive. I know that if you want me to do this, you will be there to help me.

If I shouldn't do this (if I am just trying to push something on people that they don't want), let it fall by the wayside and let me lose interest.

A beautiful peace came over me, similar to what I felt when I decided to marry David. It lasted all the way home.

The next morning I called the director of the Pleasant Grove High School team that won the National Championships. Elaine Grenko was very happy to answer my questions. She said they practiced before school. The students paid a yearly costume fee, but the costumes stayed with the team to use over and over again as they were very expensive. They added a few every year. Her team performed in her area and put on a concert each spring. She gave me a good idea of what it would take to handle such a group.

When David came home for lunch, I approached him on the subject. He was skeptical, afraid it would take time away from our children. My rebuttal was that it would give our children the opportunity to learn how to dance and also give other teenagers some of the joy we had.

I asked if he would be willing to get our younger children off to school while I was teaching. He said he did not mind doing that but felt I should teach only Monday, Wednesday, and Friday, so I would have some mornings at home. He suggested I speak with the principal to see what he thought.

Ecstatic at my husband's favorable reaction, I phoned the principal, Al Koch.

"Hello, Al. This is Alexis Beckstead. Remember me? I am Dr. Beckstead's wife."

In his German accent, Al said, "Of course, I remember seeing you and your husband dance in town many years ago. You used to be on the BYU Ballroom Dance Team, weren't you?"

"Yes," I answered. Then I took a breath and went on. "How would you feel if I started a ballroom dance team at the high school? It would be like a club?"

"I think that would be fantastic!" exclaimed Al. "Would you and your husband teach it?"

"My husband feels he is too busy with his practice, but I would be willing to volunteer my time," I told him.

"Great! But how can we get these students excited about this?" Al queried. "We need them to see how wonderful this program can be."

"The Utah schools have had success. I saw many high school teams at the National Championships this weekend. They were amazing."

"Say," exclaimed Al. "Maybe we can get the winning team to come up and put on an assembly for our school. Then we could ask the interested students to tryout," He suggested.

"That's a great idea," I agreed.

Al continued, "I'll tell you what. You call the director of this group and see if they can come, and I will work on finding money to help pay their busing costs."

"It's a deal," I agreed. "I'll let you know what she says. Thank you so much, Al."

"Oh, I think this would be a fantastic thing for our students. The more they become involved in good things, the less trouble they get into. I'll talk to you later."

Elaine's group agreed to come. The day of the assembly materialized, and the gymnasium was packed with the 750 pupils that made up our high school. When Al Koch introduced Elaine Grenko and her National Championship team, I watched the crowd intently. The students seemed to perk up at the introduction.

Out came the dancers—smiling, poised, well-trained youth who loved what they did. The music was exciting, pulling the audience in. The group not only performed those familiar dance steps, which I recognized, but they also had formations and lifts the audience cheered for. They danced medleys, the samba, cha-cha, quickstep, waltz, and many more.

Looking at the crowd again to feel out their response, I noticed some of the school's hard cases in the corner—the type that usually nothing interests. Even they were hooked, staring with envy at the young men twirling those pretty girls.

The group kept the audience captive for forty-five minutes and ended with their award winning James Bond Medley. When the men all fell down dead, the crowd stood and applauded.

Al came to the microphone. "Okay, students. We want to thank Elaine Grenko's team for coming today. Weren't they fantastic? Let's give them another hand."

The students whooped and hollered.

Al went on. "Alexis Beckstead is going to start such a team at our high school. If any of you would be interested in trying out, please sign up at the school office."

Walking over to me, Al said, "I think this will do the trick, Alexis. How could they not love this and want to be involved?"

Later after school at the office window, I called out to the secretary, "How many students signed up?"

"One hundred and twenty. I'd say there is a real interest for ballroom dancing," she commented as she handed me the list.

My steps were light as I approached my car. Closing my eyes, I whispered, "Well, Lord, it looks like you want me to do this." I opened my lids and spoke to the image in the car window. Those twelve dance classes you took at BYU are going to come in handy after all."

In the *Preston Citizen* that week, there was a picture of a ballroom couple from Elaine's team with the headline, "Beckstead Brings in Ballroom Dancing."

Chapter 15

Early Success

My first concern was to get a refresher course on the steps. I knew it was like riding a bike, a review bringing back all my training. I talked David into attending the Brigham Young University Adult Ballroom Dance Camp with me in the summer. We were amazed at the hundreds of adults from all over the country who came at great expense, taking vacation time to learn this craft. Many told us that they looked forward to it all year. It was like stepping back in time to our college days as we moved around the campus ballroom. Our relationship was enlivened like a watered plant. We especially enjoyed the American foxtrot, taught by BYU director, Lee Wakefield. The instruction I received and the video I bought provided important material I could share with my new dance team.

When I showed up early for the high school tryout, there were several young men waiting anxiously to be let in. One good-looking, young man introduced himself as Bill Swann. He had curly brown hair, a ruddy complexion, and an inviting smile. "Are you Neal Swann's son?" I asked.

"Yes. My father taught your husband how to dance" he owned proudly. "I recruited a few of my friends. We are seniors."

"It is nice to meet you," I said. "You know, I might not have met my husband, if your dad hadn't taught that class."

"Yeah, so I figured."

I conducted the tryout much like the one at BYU and, at the principal's suggestion, arranged for dance teachers from another town to judge. Al said it would save me a lot of phone calls from disappointed parents asking why I didn't pick their children—a good scapegoat. He was very wise. I posted the list of those accepted and called my new dancers that night telling them when and where to meet for practices before school. My freshman son, Dave, was among those chosen by the judges and he agreed to help me demonstrate steps in class.

At our first official meeting, I explained to the students what was expected of them and began to get the men's measurements for costumes. The boys had a competition going to see who had the biggest chest size. Regardless of my trying to keep the numbers from them, they kept looking over my shoulder and cheered each time a measurement passed up the record. The girl's measurements were done in a more private setting.

After dividing the students into a Standard and Latin team, I went to town educating them. I remembered Sue Jensen's fast-moving, teaching style and attempted to mimic it, covering technique as I went along. The noise and confusion of two teams made me realize I needed an assistant. Until I could find help, my captains kept them running through things while I alternated with the groups. Meanwhile, I kept my eyes open for another teacher.

Our teenagers' enthusiasm was like electricity in the air. I taught the Viennese waltz first, wondering if they would think it was too old-fashioned. But I was pleasantly surprised to see them put their hearts into it. The Viennese waltz was always one of my favorites, probably because of the big movement.

One day the partner of a huge, muscular boy named Mike was absent, so I filled in to make it easier for him. We came to the ending pose where he was supposed to throw me from a closed position to a side-by-side, low lung line. As my feet left the floor, I let out a yelp.

"What?" asked Mike. "Didn't I do it right?"

"Oh you did it right. But you threw me ten feet."

He had the strength of Hercules. I used to love lifts when I was young, but now as a middle-aged woman…?

"Mike, I decided I'm too old for such aerial maneuvers. I'm not filling in any more."

He laughed—proud of his ability to stun his teacher.

Besides choreography and teaching, I knew that beautiful costuming was essential to the success of our performances. For the ladies to dance without a pretty dress would be like Cinderella going to the ball in rags. I had kept in contact over the years with my friend Becky from the BYU team, who had become a professional seamstress and lived in Provo. I gave her a call, and she agreed to make eight ballroom gowns. They had peach-brocade bodices and five white layers of sparkling organza, perfect for the Viennese waltz.

The girls were full of animation when they came to my house to try them on, taking turns running up and down my grand, curved staircase for no other reason than to enjoy how they swished. Nothing makes a girl feel more feminine than an elegant dress. Eventually, I was able to get tuxedos for the men.

Keeping my eyes open for possible soloists to make an adequate show, I noticed that Bill Swann and a girl named Michelle were especially graceful. When I asked them if they would be willing to come in before class to learn a slow waltz solo, Bill nodded happily, while Michelle acted like I had just crowned her Miss Idaho.

They caught on quickly to a simplified version of an International Style routine David and I had learned in college, their elegant flow striking a soft spot in my heart.

Meanwhile, I choreographed an exuberant swing for the Latin team. My efforts were all worthwhile as I observed my son Dave have a marvelous time. This dance team was making dreams come true for Neal Swann and me—our sons were learning to dance.

Knowing how people love a lift number, I couldn't leave that out. For my first attempt I chose Mike, who was over six feet tall, built like a tank, and a member of the wrestling team. I matched him up with a small, poised girl named Audrey. His great strength and her lithe gracefulness brought images of figure skaters to mind as Mike twirled her overhead.

It dawned on me that men get some sort of masculine thrill from lifting females, while young girls love to soar through the air "with the greatest of ease." If a dance did not have a few lifts or drops, the students were disappointed, so I tried to add these to each dance to keep everyone happy.

Once established, we never lacked for performance opportunities. The principal assigned us to dance at basketball halftimes, and it was common for people to say they enjoyed the halftime better than the game. Numbers were requested for community events, church parties, and school assemblies, averaging one performance a week.

I decided to choreograph a medley number for each team to give the students experience with different rhythms and keep their interest.

Noticing another talented girl in our group named Annie, I decided to have her make an entrance as a bride in our Standard medley, which used music from a movie about a marriage. I decided to have her wear my wedding gown and veil for her costume. However, it needed some adjustments. Always glad my mother taught me to sew, I altered and hemmed often. When Annie came over to my house to be fitted, she said, "Alexis, I can't believe you would let me use your dress."

"Well, Annie, I only wore it to two receptions and I might as well get some use out of it. There are no guarantees my daughters will want to wear it later on."

The number was very clever, beginning with the team dancing around to a waltz and foxtrot. Then, Annie soared into the middle while being lifted by two tuxedoed males. She took turns dancing with four men, spinning and leaping like Rita Hayworth in an old musical. The other couples swarmed around her for a remarkable ending pose.

Wanting to continue to use Annie's talents, I also taught her a rumba solo along with a good-looking, senior boy. The rumba—a slow-moving, romantic dance—requires shifting of weight to create a lovely hip movement. I didn't have the costume finished for her first performance, so Annie wore her own wrap-around skirt that night, an alternative with shocking consequences.

As her number began, we were stunned when the button at her waist popped off. Poor Annie, not knowing what to do, was torn between holding onto her skirt or using her arms as the routine required. When she did the latter, the audience watched the fabric slowly unwind. Before it fell, she'd wrap it back up only to have it unwind again. Sometimes she resorted to using her hips to keep it on, swinging her thighs, making the dance more exotic. It was hilarious, but mortifying for Annie.

Our first year we received many invitations from other high school groups to become involved in their competitions, causing me to take a serious look at the part I wanted competitions to play in my program. For some high schools it was top priority to participate in as many competitions as they could. But these activities cost money and we had limited funds. I didn't want to spend all my free time doing fundraisers.

Time was also a consideration, especially since we were in big demand for performances in the schools and community from our very first year. I didn't want distant obligations interfering with my students joining the band, maybe choir, the school play, or participating in a sport. Multiple activities would help them stay well rounded. I didn't think dancing should be their only focus, especially this early in their lives.

Performing was service oriented, a win-win situation—the audience and performers both winners. Competitions, on the other hand, had winners and losers. It could be frustrating not to receive recognition. I knew, however, that competitions could encourage the students to improve themselves. I worried that a program based solely on competitions would teach students to look for the elusive greener pasture—"I'll only be happy when I get that medal." I wanted students to know that they could find all the joy and satisfaction dance had to offer in their own backyard. Remembering my past experience, the greatest time I had while dancing was not winning a competition. It was performing. Making people happy was what it was all about to me. I knew there was a place for competitions, but moderation was the key.

After considering all the issues, I opted to do one main team competition a year—the Gem State Invitational. It included high schools in Idaho, Utah, Wyoming, and Nevada, giving my students an opportunity to see what other groups were doing, as well as motivation to improve themselves.

To sum it all up, I felt that it was about balance. Balance brings happiness, and that's what I wanted for my students.

For our concert at the end of the first year, my husband agreed to perform an International foxtrot with me. We practiced at the church gym in the evenings, and it was like old times running through our school routines together. I was pleasantly surprised when rehearsing brought out David's romantic side. He suddenly slipped his arms around me and kissed my neck and lips passionately.

Struggling to free myself, I said. "David, what if the Bishop walks in? It would be so embarrassing."

He stopped, looked over his shoulder, and said, "Let him walk in," then continued as before.

My solo gown created by Becky rivaled a spectacular Blackpool dress with a burgundy bodice and layered, black skirt covered with rhinestones and trimmed with feathers.

To advertise for the concert, I put an article in the newspaper and hung flyers around the town, as well as in my husband's office.

The night of the show, it was good to be a performer again, dancing with the man I loved. The students did all their numbers with enthusiasm, then, came together for a big finale to a song about making people happy. I thought it was appropriate, since that is what dancing is all about to me.

After our concert, I was mobbed by grateful parents overjoyed with their son or daughter's participation. Many of David's patients said they came just to see him dance. A dozen people commented, "I wish we had this when I was in high school."

One mother shared something significant to her. "Alexis, when our family moved to Preston at the beginning of the school year, my daughter, didn't know anyone. I was really concerned for her happiness. Then she got involved in your group and immediately made thirty-six friends. I owe you so much for giving her this experience. She now feels at home in this community and would never want to move back to our old town."

I told the woman how much I loved her daughter.

Al came up to congratulate me. He spoke about one senior boy on my team in particular named Chris. "You know, Chris has never done anything in high school—no sports, plays, band or choir. It was so good to see him involved tonight. I am going to see if I can budget you more club money next year, Alexis."

"Thank you, Al. I couldn't have done it without your support."

The first Preston High Standard Dance Team

Chapter 16

Fabulous Fun

It was kismet when I went to "Back to School Night" the beginning of my second year of teaching. A new grade school teacher named Heather Brown was introduced, and my internal radar went off when they announced she had been on a high school ballroom team in Sandy, Utah for four years. Afterward, I approached her and asked about her dance background, she described her training and love of dancing with a spark in her eye. I explained my need for an assistant, and she willingly accepted. Her contribution made all the difference.

About this time, a man named Mr. Bright passed away. He had been raised in Preston, graduated from our high school many years before, and had become financially successful.

In his will he arranged for $500,000 dollars to be put in a trust fund to help Preston High. Each year the interest on the money was to be divided among the fine arts groups to help build their programs. The Bright Fund was responsible for many improvements, such as, the addition of the orchestra program at our school, and funds to pay my ballroom assistant.

We did some fabulous numbers over the many years to follow. As choreographers, my assistant and I tried to keep the interest of the participants by including a variety of dances. We used the five Latin dances—cha-cha, jive, paso doble, samba, and rumba—as well as the five Standard dances. Sometimes we mixed the program up with a two-step, west coast swing, Lindy hop, Charleston, New York hustle, hip hop, polka, or mambo. Because of that variety, I never tired of teaching. Each dance had something unique about it that made me feel something different.

The swing was very popular and fit energetic teens like a glove. One morning I worked on finishing our 50's medley and told the students standing around, "Now, for the ending move I want all of you to get ready to hit your pose, while Mike and Brooke do a waterfall."

"What's a waterfall?" asked Brooke, a petite, brunette.

I moved them over to a mat and got spotters. "You stand here facing each other. Brooke, you run toward Mike as he bends over. Diving over his back, your head goes through his legs, and he pulls you up to face him again," I explained.

"You want my head to go where?" Brooke asked. How is he supposed to pull me up?

"He will hold onto your legs with one hand and your neck with the other."

"This is scary!" she exclaimed, "But I'll try." She stepped away for a distance and started to run. Jumping on his back, she found herself looking at his behind. She closed her eyes and flinched. He struggled to find the proper handhold as she came over. With Mike not knowing how to support her legs, she rolled to the floor flat on her back.

She lay still and silent for a few seconds, then, giggled. After a sigh of regret she got up to try again. This time as she went over, I grabbed Mike's hand and showed him where to hold her legs. They made it on the next attempt.

"This is going to take awhile to do it fast, but we will get it. Don't you worry, Alexis," declared Mike.

Later that month in the high school gym packed with people for a basketball game, the team walked out onto the floor after the second quarter. The bouncing music started and so did the swing dancers. They moved around in formations as they triple stepped, spinning and twirling. The first group did kick steps to exit. Another team made an entrance with each man leaping over a standing girl's head to the rippling sound of the music. The girls fell back, the boys caught them under their arms, turned the girls to step over their bodies, and threw the girls back up in a jump. They were having the time of their lives.

Almost over now, Brooke ran toward Mike and did a speedy somersault over his back and up his front. Mike grabbed Brooke under her arms, spun her in a circle and set her on the floor hitting a pose, while two other boys ran for a body slide crisscrossing on the floor to the phrase, "Goodness gracious, great balls of fire!" The audience erupted into applause and cheers. The swing number was just one example of the excitement we stirred in a crowd.

Losing my seniors from the previous year was hard, but returning students now had a year of experience under their belts. K'Lyn and Brett were doing exceptionally well, so I invited them to learn a Viennese waltz solo.

They were nervous but excited the first night they were to perform the number. When the tall, stunning couple came forward—Brett in a classic tuxedo with tails and K'Lyn dressed in a long, pink gown with her hair done up like a model—they couldn't help but command attention. Slowly, the music began filling the room with the haunting refrain of "The Blue Danube," by Strauss.

The gentleman bowed and she curtseyed. Taking his hand, K'Lyn ran around Brett gracefully holding out her chiffon folds. Spinning into dance position, they were off into the world of the Viennese waltz with right and left turns, checks and spins, fall-away runs, and change-of-place explosions to name a few. The rhythm tempted the audience to sway to and fro. He twirled her up into lifts with graceful flair. Goosebumps went up my spine as the dance came to a close, giving me the best payoff I could ask for after all my hours of work.

In the hall after the performance, K'Lyn's father approached me. "How can I thank you?" he asked. "It was so wonderful to see my daughter out there looking like a queen and experiencing this kind of beauty." He got choked up and tears filled his eyes as he said, "I love her so much. Thank you for what you have done for my daughter."

I reflected on the time I spent with these two, fine people listening to that marvelous classical tune morning after morning, watching their enthusiasm build for the great art of dance, and responded with sincerity, "It was a privilege."

Unfortunately, performances didn't always go the way we wanted them to. A girl named Jane on the Standard team struggled to keep up in the polka. We were in for a surprise at a basketball game one night. The gym was almost full to capacity when an announcer's voice blared over the loudspeaker, "Ladies and Gentlemen, for your halftime entertainment, the Preston High School Ballroom Dance Team." The crowd cheered as the group walked on dressed in Polish attire. A lively accordion revved them up for polka turns, then, heel-toe slides to a horizontal line. Half the line turned the opposite direction to pivot the line counterclockwise. The audience began to clap in time. While the eight men grabbed each other's wrists and formed a ring, the girls backed into the men to sit on the gentlemen's arms. The boys lifted the girls and walked in a circle. Suddenly, Jane lost her balance and fell backwards. Her dress flew up as she went into an upside down position hanging by her bent knees. As the boys walked and the girls waved, everyone in the room got a clear view of Jane's panties. The people made a sound of alarm as she fell, then the whole room roared with laughter at the silly scene.

Later when I saw Jane in the hall, I took her by the shoulders and said, "I can't believe you hung on so long."

She explained, "My partner told me to fall off, but I refused to avoid getting hurt."

In saving her back, Jane didn't realize the dignity she lost.

Sometimes embarrassing things happened at the practices. One morning I announced that I needed to measure the boys' biceps for Charleston armbands. As they came, I asked each one to flex his arm in order to get the biggest measurement, so it would not be too tight.

What a silly situation it turned out to be. The boys rolled up their sleeves and

gloried in showing off their muscles to the wide-eyed, drooling girls. Then Mike came forward to show them all up. He was a good-looking monster with biceps that seemed the size of tetherballs. The girls made oohing and aahing sounds as he flexed. I, too, was shocked at his arms and found myself saying, "My goodness,

Mike. I can't believe you!" He grinned and blushed, loving every minute of the attention.

When we finished, I announced, "Okay, let's run through the Charleston. Everyone get in your places."

At that point Mike rolled up his pant legs and his other sleeve and began to dance. He dramatized every move melodramatically. "How do you like my costume, Alexis?" he yelled. The sight was so funny seeing this big hulk do the Charleston in his ridiculous pants that I laughed until tears came.

That routine included the airplane—where the dancers alternated kicking their feet to the side and touching them with arms extended like wings. Then the boys pretended to kiss the girls. In response, the ladies swung to hit the men while the men ducked. It was a cute routine.

Another popular dance was the cha-cha, with its step-together-step motion. Autumn, a senior, was establishing herself as a talented Latin dancer. I paired her up with another senior for a cha-cha solo. I had a special red dress made for her with black polka dots and a hem of diagonal cut ruffles. Their rhythmic dance, performed with enthusiasm, was well received. That year I had T-shirts made for the team with the words, "Dance or Die." I thought the saying had particular reference to Autumn. At the end of the year I received a special note from her:

Dear Alexis,

It used to be that I had no clue what Ballroom even was. You don't know how much I'm going to miss it. Thank you for letting me dance the cha-cha. I loved it. I guess if we had to choose between dancing or dying, we'd dance forever. I feel sorry for people who never dance. That is why I'm grateful for you. Now I live a more spicy life.

Little did I know what it would mean to teach that little, blond fireball to dance.

Swing dancers

Chapter 17

My Dancing Children

My son Dave loved to dance! He was a shy, timid person of average height, but he would light up like a fourth of July celebration when he moved on the floor. His excellent rhythm made him particularly good at Latin. My college trip to Blackpool and Europe couldn't give me more happiness than it did to watch Dave enjoy himself at rehearsals and performances.

Dave was equally talented at cross-country running and singing. He had a beautiful voice. I know that success in these areas also added to his self-esteem. However, ballroom dancing seemed to help him socially more than anything else. I watched him come out of his shell and learn to talk to girls, making many friends.

For the first part of high school, Dave had a thing for disco. It made a short comeback among teenagers at that time. When a visiting professional, Rick Robinson, was at Utah State University for a workshop we were attending, I asked him to choreograph a disco duet, which included Dave. It was a hot number. Whenever the two couples came out in their bellbottoms and sequined shirts doing John Travolta moves, the crowd went crazy. It made me happy to see my son feeling like a superstar.

When Dave was a senior, I asked the Preston Junior High principal if he would be interested in having Dave and I teach a ballroom class as an elective to the eighth graders. The principal was very agreeable, and we had no problem getting enough people to sign up. They put sixty students, including my daughter, Laura, in my class with many more on a waiting list. I eventually had to cut the class down to a more realistic size of thirty because of the noise, but I was glad there was such an interest.

I learned immediately about the short attention span of thirteen and fourteen year olds. Dave came over from the high school to be my aid and received credit for it. We demonstrated a few steps, turned the music on to get their attention, and started counting. By the end of the semester they had learned about ten short routines, which they did well. I decided my forte was working with high school students, but that class had allowed me to prepare some people for my tryouts. It was also the beginning of a group of friends that would be bonded for life through dance.

Because of his competence, I arranged for Dave to do a cha-cha solo with Rachael, who was also gifted. It was a complex routine with demanding, syncopated moves. They performed it many times, including for the floorshow of a church ball. The number was a success, but after the show I learned just how advanced Dave had become as an impromptu dancer.

When the band started playing a foot-stomping melody, I watched in amazement as Dave led a girl named Joanna through a fabulous swing where he hardly used any move more than once, and every transition was executed flawlessly. Their faces were lit up with smiles. Joanna followed superbly. It was pure joy to watch, making me think of my college days when my husband and I boogied to "In the Mood."

Taking a deep breath, I mentally patted myself on the back. I had done what I set out to do and taught my son how to really live.

When Wesley, my second son, became a freshman in high school, he declared adamantly, "You're not going to turn me into a ballroom dancer. Ballroom is for 'wooses,'" his term for a momma's boy. Wesley emphatically fought my suggestion that he tryout.

"Do you think Mike is a woose?" I reasoned.

"Well, Mike is different. He's cool," Wes argued. "But you should hear the jocks talk about the ballroom kids. They think they are strange and stuck-up."

"They're just jealous," I contradicted. "What guy wouldn't want to dance with a cute girl and throw her around?"

Wes shook his head, "Well, I'm not going to do it, anyway. I'd rather be involved in sports. My goal is to be on the basketball team."

He would not listen to my argument that he could do sports as well as dance, like many of the students on my team. I was disappointed that he did not want to learn what I loved best.

"I still love you even though you don't want to dance, Wes. I just wanted you to have all the fun that I've had in life."

"I'll have plenty of fun, Mom. Don't worry about me."

Having picked up the habit of writing poetry from my father, I wrote a limerick about

Wes in my spare time that expressed what he was missing.

> There once was a boy named Wesley
> Who didn't like ballroom sadly.
> Because he won't dance,
> He misses his chance
> To have women around constantly.

When Wes was a sophomore, he took a weightlifting class and became impressed with his expanding muscles. I often found him posed in front of the mirror flexing his six-foot tall frame. One day he called me into the family room and said, "Hey, Mom, I can do a lift routine. Watch." He then hoisted his little brother over his head in a T-press. Good thing we had a high ceiling.

"Very good, Wes," I praised. "But wouldn't it be more fun with a cute girl?"

Another day my children called me into the same room to see them copy a move we did in ballroom. Two boys held their youngest sister in the air by the shoulders while another held her feet up so she was parallel to the floor. They walked her all over the room like she was the main dish at a banquet. My children attempted many different lifts over the years with one another—each a comedy.

I had to admit that I liked basketball games more with Wes on the team.

Even though I had given up hope that Wesley would learn to dance, fate had a surprising twist. At the end of his junior year, Wes asked a lovely girl to go to the prom with him. Each year for the Prom, the Student Exec Council organized a floorshow dance number called the "promenade" for any interested couples. Not everyone participated, but Wes' date got him to dance with her. They looked adorable together and Wes seemed to enjoy himself.

At the beginning of Wes' senior year, I was shocked when he approached me in a very humble manner and said, "Mom, I'm kind of afraid to tell you this." He frowned. "You know Bracken on your team?"

"Yes."

"She talked me into doing a dance. I am going to be in a lift routine for the Homecoming assembly. Can you believe it? The Exec Council asked Bracken to choreograph it."

"Wes, I am so happy! They came through where I failed. It's astonishing what a young man will do for the feminine sex."

"Mom, that isn't all. We had our first practice after school today, and it was so much fun! No wonder you wanted me to dance."

The turn of events was such a surprise. I had led my horse to water, but only a filly could make him drink.

That wasn't the end of it. When my church leaders asked me to teach a dance to our youth group for the floorshow of a church ball, Wes and my daughter Laura decided that they wanted to be partners. Recalling all the fighting they had done over the years, I expressed my shock that they would pair off together. "Well, Mom," replied Laura. "Considering who else there is to dance with, I think we made the best choice."

We ended up with about eight couples and worked on the number once a week for two months. In the meantime, Bracken had rounded up Wes and five basketball players to dance a swing she choreographed to "Boogie Woogie Bugle Boy." I couldn't believe it when I saw the tough jocks bounce around with the energetic girls at the high school assembly. It was obvious they were having a great time. When word got out about their cute dance, they were asked to perform it at the church ball.

The gym was bustling with people the night of the dance. When it was time for my youth group to go on, I signaled the sound people to start the music.

"Ba, Ba, Baaa, Ba, Barbara Ann!" Half the kids bobbed up and down alternating. Then the other half repeated before they went into full swing. I videotaped as Wes scooped up my tiny Laura, threw her feet around his back, grabbed her legs, dropped her shoulders, and swung her body around to the front where Wes caught her in a cradle position. She was flying.

A few minutes later, Wes and his basketball buddies began their "Boogie Woogie Bugle Boy" showpiece. I laughed at the thought of my non-dancing son getting finagled into being a teenybopper. In the hall when it was over, he confided to me again that he loved dancing.

Although Wes never did try out for my ballroom team in high school, he ended up getting plenty of dancing in his senior year. Thanks to the fillies.

Wes reminded me of a boy named Mac. Mac came reluctantly to our tryout one year with a foreign exchange student whom his family was hosting. The German was determined to tryout and Mac conceded he would tag along to keep the visitor happy. It was plain to see that Mac didn't want to be there, but endured patiently as I started the first dance. Into the second dance, I noticed a change in Mac. He no longer looked bored and annoyed. He was smiling and enthusiastic. Being very coordinated, Mac made the team. Unfortunately, his German friend did not. Mac went on to catch the ballroom bug and was faithful year after year. He ended up doing several specialties and a gorgeous slow waltz his senior year. All that from a boy who initially made up his mind that he would hate ballroom dancing.

When my son Dave went to Brigham Young University as a freshman, he made the Summer Ballroom Team and enjoyed that experience. Eventually, however, he decided to put his largest effort into singing, which did not bother me one bit. He had a fabulous voice, and I loved going to his choir performances. However, I was very happy that he did not neglect taking some dance classes as well. He increased his pool of steps, technique, and his ability to make up any dance when called upon with a worthy follower.

One semester he called with some exciting news, "Hey, Mom, you will never guess what happened! My partner and I won first place in the intermediate swing at the BYU Dancesport Competition."

"Hooray!" I said. I thought of the night he and Joanna ripped up the floor and was not surprised at all.

Chapter 18

For the Kids

When my assistant, Heather, moved away after a couple of years, I was lucky to enlist the help of Misty Porter. She had moved to Franklin upon marrying a boy from the area. Having been a member of the Utah State Ballroom Dance Team, she was a superb dance teacher for my group for the next three years. She made up some excellent routines. Her sweet and kind personality made the students immediately adore her.

I learned a lot from Misty, especially in how she interacted with the students. She would quietly watch them go through a sequence. Afterward, she would gather them around her and praise them for the good things they did. Then she would point out a few areas where they could do better and had them work on those parts. She never got angry, but was as "patient as the day is long" (to use a borrowed phrase from my farmer). The teenagers loved her and wanted to try hard to make her happy. Over the years, if I found myself being too critical, I tried to remember Misty and her complimentary ways. She was a good example to me.

As I taught, I found I had other lessons to learn. One came through Mrs. Rogers and her daughter.

The doorbell rang at my home not long after tryouts, and I went to answer it. "Hello Mrs. Rogers," I greeted. "How are you?"

"I'm fine," she answered and then added, "Would you mind if I talk to you for a few minutes?"

"Not at all," I replied and asked her to come in and sit down. I knew exactly why she had come. Her daughter, Tina, who had been on my team last year, was not chosen this fall.

Mrs. Rogers started in, "It is about Tina. She is heartbroken she didn't make the team. I've never seen her so unhappy. Why was she good enough for last year, but not this year?"

"I'm sorry, but the judges didn't pick her," I informed her.

"But Mrs. Beckstead, isn't this whole thing about kids rather than how good they are?"

"Mrs. Rogers, I have to keep the quality of dancing high, so people will want to watch us perform and students will desire to be part of it."

"I understand that," she responded with a sad look. "But can't you use her someway? Can she be your assistant? Anything, just to have her involved in this great program."

"Sure, I could do that," I replied. I often need fill-ins when some of the students can't make performances. Go ahead and tell her to come and I'll find a way to use her."

"Oh, you don't know how happy that will make her," expressed the concerned mother. "Thank you, from the bottom of my heart."

Tina was a sweet girl, and I was happy to have her back. She seemed to hold no grudge and was willing to help anyway she could. As it turned out, one student was in a car accident and had to quit dancing while she recovered. Tina learned her spot and did a great job, another year of practice improving Tina's skills.

The year went fast, and Tina was an important part of it. After our spring concert, her mother approached me, and I humbly said, "Mrs. Rogers, I had to learn my lesson. You were right. These kids are far more important than the program."

She smiled, and thanked me for letting her daughter have this great experience.

Thinking long and hard about how I could include more students, I shared my concerns with the director of the BYU-Idaho Dance Team, Shawn Fisher, when I had the opportunity to speak to him one day.

"One of the biggest problems I have to deal with, Shawn, is having to turn so many teenagers away. We have nearly a hundred students tryout every year, and I can only keep thirty-six. These students watch us perform at the grade school as children and grow up with the goal to ballroom dance in high school. By the time they get to ninth grade, they are devastated if they don't make the team."

He gave me a great suggestion. "Start a backup team and have your seniors teach it. That's what high schools around here do. More kids can dance, and it gives your students leadership experience. Ask a parent to supervise."

Feeling like I scored on a TV game show, I said. "I think that's the answer, Shawn. I'm going to do it."

A willing parent oversaw the new team. Now, almost fifty teenagers a year could dance, and it was helping students develop teaching and leadership skills.

As I continued to instruct, I learned the importance of being sensitive to the needs of the students I worked with. One day after rehearsal, June and Ryan came up to me.

"Alexis, we would like to do a country swing solo."

"I'm sorry, but I don't know much about that dance," I confessed.

"We have learned a few steps. Let us show you what we can do and maybe you could figure something out."

They demonstrated some very impressive dance steps and wild lifts I had never seen before.

"Wow, you are really good at this. Let me search through my old videos to get some ideas. With what you know, we might be able to put something together."

"Cool!" they said and ran with a few hops out the gym door, looking like children on their way to a candy store.

I had enough solo numbers but I was aware that this couple had been going through some disappointing times. I had asked June's younger sister, a talented Latin dancer, to do a specialty with my son Dave that year. It had been hard for June to be passed over in favor of her less-experienced sister. And Ryan had tried out for the lead in the school play, but my same son got the part over Ryan. So both students had every reason to be angry with the solo couple that year. Instead of acting resentful, they sought an opportunity to express their own talents. Knowing what they were going through, I could not turn them down.

The results were worth the extra effort it took me to learn about an unfamiliar dance. Together we created a unique crowd pleaser. Dressed in jeans and colorful shirts, June and Ryan did all kinds of pretzel-type, arm-ducking twirls. Their tricky lifts were a smash. One was called the can opener where Ryan picked June up in cradle position, she flipped a leg around his head, he turned her upside-down, and she swung her free leg around under his arm to scissor his shoulder upside-down while he held her two hands and spun.

In another move, he pulled June through his legs. She did a backward somersault to wrap her legs around his waist, and with her torso parallel to the floor, he spun her in a circle holding onto her hands. A moment later she jumped onto Ryan piggyback style then rotated to his front. It was unbelievable that she could hold with her legs wrapped around his middle as she lay out flat while he spun her. Throughout the dance the audience clapped to the rhythm and cheered wildly. Ryan and June were in the spotlight achieving success. Now their senior year was a triumph. Working together to bring an exciting new dance to our audiences, gave me confidence to try an eight-couple country swing the following year. I was stretching and learning new things, too. Even if it was all for the kids.

Chapter 19

Coming to Life

Dozens of young people came to life through ballroom dance. Some personalities actually seemed to change as they gained new skills. One teenager that stands out in my mind is Josh. Josh was a very serious young man when he first joined the team—a realist. He described situations the way he saw them, and it wasn't through rose-colored glasses. But soon I detected an alteration. Latin dancing with pretty girls seemed to cheer him up, and make him smile more.

Because of his personality, I had a feeling Josh might really get into the paso doble. The paso is a very serious dance. It imitates a matador swinging his cape around with the woman representing the cape.

I asked Josh if he would like to be part of a four-couple paso doble specialty. He accepted and was willing to come at 6:30 in the mornings, a half hour before regular class. As I taught the dramatic, staccato steps, Josh took on the posture of a real matador, eating it up. He kept an appropriate scowl on his face throughout, which often made me crack a smile. He stomped around, threw his arms upward, did snappy dips with his partner, and whipped her through his legs for a theatrical pose.

One day after class Josh could hold it in no longer. The skepticism dissolved. "Man, I love the paso doble. It is my favorite dance!"

He went to sit down by his partner, Melissa, which he had been doing a lot lately. Maybe it wasn't *only* the paso he liked.

Toward the end of the year we put on assemblies for the elementary and junior high schools. As we waited between shows, I saw Josh sitting on the floor surrounded by six Standard girls in their fluffy white ballroom gowns gathered close around him in a circle. He was blooming with all the attention. "Why Josh, you look like a flower," I suggested.

A smiling one at that, I thought. Josh hadn't looked solemn for quite a while.

One September at our first rehearsal, I noticed a new member named Stephanie who had come in as a sophomore. She was a tall, beautiful brunette with a charming smile. But she looked self conscious about some marks on her skin. When I walked up to her, she immediately explained that the half-inch, red spots all over her body were from a recent illness. "No one needs to worry. They are not contagious. They are supposed to go away soon," she assured me.

I expressed my sympathy and said that her spots did not matter one bit to anyone here. She seemed relieved. Her Standard dance partner was very kind to her and did not act repelled. In a few weeks Stephanie's spots were gone and she seemed to feel better about herself.

In April of that year, I ran into Stephanie's mother at the grocery store. She had something to tell me. "Alexis, you will never know what being on the dance team has done for Stephanie. Mortification over her spots made her whole self-image go down the drain. But after being on your team this year, she came right out of it. Dancing built up her confidence. She found a partner to take private lessons and compete with and has even arranged to do her senior project around dance."

I expressed to Stephanie's mother that I was glad dancing had helped her daughter.

Another changed life.

Claye joined my group as a ninth grader. The first day of class he entered timidly keeping to himself. He had medium brown hair and was rather short, but I immediately noticed his rosy cheeks. When he got up to dance with the Latin team, he acted a little self-conscious, struggling to talk with his partner. However, as he loosened up on the dance floor, Claye turned into a different person and put great energy into his movements. It was clear the kid absolutely loved to dance.

Later in the year when we put on assemblies for the younger grades, I noticed Claye speaking easily with many females around him in the hall. He performed with fervor and happiness as the children cheered at every difficult move as if the teens were professionals.

Back in class, Claye no longer walked in with his head down. He smiled, waved, and joked with the others the minute he came in. This was not my shy Claye who had appeared the September before. He was a more sociable, confident individual — a much happier soul.

As Claye developed his natural dance ability, it was like watching an acorn grow into a mighty oak, and all the hot girls sought to be in his shade. In his sophomore year, a senior named Rachael invited him to do a cha-cha solo with her, which she choreographed herself. His junior year he did a fabulous paso doble solo with Tosha. When he was in twelfth grade Stephanie asked him to dance a samba as part of her senior project. I had to laugh at how the girls were drawn to this sweet, humble Latin dancer.

Did I say Latin dancer? By the time he was a senior, Claye shot up like a rocket in height over six feet tall, and I asked him if he would mind dancing on my Standard team. He looked at me in drenched disappointment. You would think I had just shot his dog. "Oh no, Alexis, please don't move me to Standard. Please. I love Latin."

"But Claye, you are so tall now. I need a tall guy to dance with the tall women. You'll like it. I promise. Please give it a try."

He agreed to do it only because he was such a nice guy and didn't want to offend me, which made me like him all the more. His dissatisfaction ended quickly when he became interested in one particular Standard girl. Sparks flew when Claye began sitting awfully close to Samantha each time he showed up for class. Initially, Claye was crushed when I transferred him to the Standard team, but it didn't last when he got a crush on Samantha. I asked the students to pick a different partner for each new number, but Claye and Samantha could not resist dancing together several times that year. Overlooking it, I chuckled to myself at how my shy freshman had become quite the lady's man and a dancing king.

After tryouts one fall, a ballroom student expressed surprise that his friend, Donovan, who made the team, would even try out. "It's funny, Alexis. Donovan is late for school a lot, sleeps in class, and doesn't care about sports. He is ho-hum about everything. I am so amazed he would get up early to dance."

I tried to respond positively, "Donovan is really coordinated, strong, and good looking. The girls are going to like dancing with him this year. Hey, he sounds like you."

Don's friend smiled and rolled his eyes.

As I began to teach, I found out Don had a mind of his own. At the end of the 70s disco medley there were sounds like gunfire, so the ladies used imaginary guns to shoot their partners. All the boys fell to the ground, except Don. "Donovan," I shouted. "You're supposed to be dead!"

"They missed me," he joked. Some days he died. Other days he did not. A few times he hobbled away like he was wounded. We never knew what he was going to do.

At our year-end concert, Don wouldn't die. He stood there like a sore thumb. Later his parents came up to me and apologized, "We appreciate all you have done to put up with our son."

I laughed, then tried to console them, "Donovan was great this year. He actually was very cooperative and we had a fun time together. You don't need to worry that he was a problem, because he wasn't."

They looked relieved. The father expressed his surprise that Don even got up for ballroom rehearsals.

"I am glad he found the motivation to come," I expressed.

"So are we," said Donovan's mother. "So are we."

Years later I ran into Donovan after he had gone to college. He was a high caliber, sharp young man. I hugged him and told him that I treasured our dance memories. He confided, "I was always glad I did ballroom dancing. It was the funnest thing I'd ever done."

Keith was another example of a young man who came to life under the influence of dance. When he became a member of the backup team, he was short and quiet, lacking confidence and dance ability. I doubted I could ever move him up. Then he became friends with a girl from the Latin team named Julia. Julia was petite like Keith, but had a great deal of ambition. She had a powerful affect on Keith. She worked with him to improve his skills on their own time, making up their own routines for a dance competition. When I saw them at the competition, I couldn't believe it was the same Keith. He had come alive with Julia as his partner.

The next year I moved Keith up to the Latin team. Boy, was he excited! As he and Julia continued to dance together, there was a whole different look about him. He came out of his shell and seemed more secure. Time on the dance floor with Julia had made the difference.

Because of his slight build, in one routine I had four girls lift him over their heads to carry him about, adding a little comedy. He was a good sport.

The summer after Keith graduated I happened to drive by the City Park and saw him teaching a couple of girls how to dance the swing. I smiled all the way home thinking of the change I had seen in him over the past four years.

An email from a dancer named Hailey best explains what ballroom could mean to a freshman:

Dear Alexis,

Thank you so much for believing in me and for the wonderful times I had this year. I don't usually wake up so early in the morning for anything, but ballroom was definitely the exception. I was nervous coming into high school as a freshman, but ballroom helped me make new friends and know that there was a place to go and already feel accepted. Ballroom is a fabulous program that you started and I am so grateful that you did. You have helped so many students. I see it in their dancing. I remember watching the ballroom team as a first grader, dreaming about being on the team when I got older. I hope to continue doing the high school team with you. It is my dream come true.

One summer Shawn Fisher, the BYU-Idaho director, put on a ballroom dance camp in Preston because of the great interest for dance in our town. He brought some experienced professionals to teach. During a break, I had the opportunity to speak with Ron Montez, seven-time American Latin Champion. I told him, "Ron, I have seen young people come into my program who are shy, introverted, and have low self-esteem; by the end of the year they are talking, have lots of friends, and dance with confidence. They feel good about themselves. The transformation is amazing!"

Ron's eyes twinkled as he responded. "I've had similar experiences with the older people I've taught. They come to my class looking worn out. They feel their prime has passed them by, and they have little to look forward to. But as they learn, their countenance changes. Their posture changes; they hold themselves up with a new vibrancy. Life is once again beautiful and sweet. They discover life hasn't passed them by and now they have a new zest for it."

I smiled and nodded. Ron and I understood each other perfectly. Any ballroom teacher would know exactly what Ron was talking about. This medium rejuvenates and gives a sense of fulfillment. Socrates, himself, felt that something was missing in his life until he took up dancing in his old age (*Xenophon, Symposium*, II, 15-20).

Josh King blooming with attention

Chapter 20

Dancing into Friendship

Our "Phantom of the Opera" number was almost ready. I had paid an experienced choreographer to teach the students, and it was coming together tremendously. The boys liked the change of working with a man and using the large black capes provided.

Couples swirled to the Viennese rhythm, first with the men clasping the capes, then with the ladies holding them up while the men spun the ladies around by the waist. It climaxed with eight girls griping arms and capes in a circle, the men lifting the whole ring of girls over their heads with locked arms, moving clockwise.

After instructing the captains to go over a few sequences again, I left to help the Latin team in the cafeteria.

Later upon returning to the gym I found a distressing sight. The Standard team was mulling around while Angela and Lisa were arguing with each other.

"We are supposed to do it like I said!" growled Angela.

"We are not. It looks better if we do it like I told you," grimaced Lisa.

"You don't know what you are talking about," said Angela sternly.

I had been gone for only a few minutes when this flared up.

"Hey, wait a minute. Stop!" I interceded, stepping between the two girls. "I don't ever, ever want this to happen. Please don't argue with each other. If you have questions, come to me and we will work it out. If we fight, then dancing is no longer fun. We've got to stay friends through this."

The girls looked at the floor in shame.

Continuing, I asked, "Now what part would you like to go over?" They explained their concern, and I straightened out the problem. After we ran through the number again, they all seemed satisfied.

I had seen this type of thing before, contentious dancing. There is no joy in it. I had witnessed dance teachers yell and growl at their students like tyrants, giving endless lectures about being quiet and had seen arguing dancers.

From the beginning I made up my mind that I wouldn't have it. By keeping the students moving and using the music to capture their attention, I found there were few problems. Dancing itself had its own cures. And like David and I discussed when we were dating, the best way to teach was with love.

Mending poor relationships and building lasting friendships, I discovered, was one of the beautiful side effects of dance.

When my daughter Laura tried out and joined my group as a freshman, I talked to her after school the same day. "Laura, I am so happy you made the team."

"Thanks, Mom. Some of the girls have been talking about who they might have to dance with. Jolene doesn't want to be partners with Dale, and Launie can't stand Dan."

"Well, that's too bad. I expect the girls to dance with all of the boys," I told her.

At our first rehearsal I spoke to the team members gathered together: "This year is a little different, you will notice, with many freshmen making the team. I taught a junior high class last year, and that means the ninth graders have as much experience as some of you already in our group."

"I want to make one thing very clear. You are all here because you can dance. Seniors will dance with freshmen, and we will treat each other as equals. I want no class distinction or talking behind each other's backs. We should all be the best of friends."

"If you have a partner who is struggling to learn, please be patient with him or her. We all get better with practice and time. You will be learning at least three numbers this year, and I would like you to have a different partner for each dance. It is a good experience to dance with many people because you can learn a lot from one another. Now, I want to see you pick partners for our medleys."

After everyone paired off, I noticed that Jolene was not Dale's partner but that Launie ended up with Dan. Launie did not look happy about it. Over the next few months they worked on an energetic swing choreographed by Misty, a dance so dynamic no one could watch it without tapping their toes. The group came out in one close, huddled mass. As the music started, they all bounced their shoulders up and down with their arms close to their sides and palms parallel to the floor. They moved to two vertical lines where the men dropped to the ground and grabbed at the girls legs as the women did kick-ball-changes away from the boys. The girls pretended to kick the boys and the men flipped back. There were passes and many popular swing steps. It was an audience favorite.

Throughout the year I overheard Launie make rude comments out loud about Dan, which I was sure he heard. I felt sorry for the boy. He seemed pretty annoyed with her. Meanwhile, Jolene did everything she could to discourage Dale from ever asking her to dance by the dirty looks she gave him. I wished I knew how to get them to be friends.

Fortunately, dancing did for them what I could not. Because of close proximity and the opportunity to see each other in a positive light, my students began to recognize the good in one another.

At the end of Laura's junior year, she came to me and confided, "Mom, Jolene told me she has been feeling so bad about the way she has treated Dale. She knows she has been really mean by giving him the cold shoulder. She decided he is a nice guy after all. When everyone was signing yearbooks today, she wrote a message in Dale's book that said, 'I'm sorry for being such a jerk to you. I think you are a great guy. Please forgive me.'"

"He didn't say anything about it but went up to her later and talked for a few minutes. Jolene told me she feels so much better about herself. She is glad they are friends now."

"Oh, Laura," I rejoiced. "I am so pleased to hear that. I am very fond of Dale."

In class toward the end of the same year, Launie and Dan walked into the gym with their arm around the other, talking like they were best buddies. I asked myself, Is this the same couple that seemed to hate each other as freshmen? Things sure had changed. Dancing had made them friends.

Lindy Hop Friends

Laura was part of a close-knit group of eighteen ballroom friends that were in my eighth-grade dance class and ended up on the high school team their freshman year. They took turns arranging parties at their homes and traded around dating. The boys made sure the girls in their crowd had dates for any special school dance, and the girls did the same for the boys in regards to girls' choice.

Word came back to me that Laura's group was changing the school and church dances. I observed this for myself one New Year's Eve while waiting for our floorshow performance and could not believe my eyes. My ballroom students made requests of the disc jockey to play danceable tunes and taught their friends around them how do the cha-cha, swing, and samba. They even got the music man to play a polka.

They traded partners often and stirred up the dance floor. I watched as a large group of teenagers formed a circle. One person would move to the center, make up a creative gyration, and everyone copied. Then the next person would dream up something. It was a great way to get everyone involved, my students being the bravest and most willing to risk. It was wonderful to see others discovering the fun.

While ballroom students reached out to others at school dances, in class they were becoming unified through performing numbers. Laura was a sophomore when September eleventh came—the unforgettable day when terrorists crashed planes into the Pentagon and World Trade Center. Patriotism spread over the country like wildfire. Flags were everywhere in homes, businesses, and car windows. My own love of country being stirred, I decided to choreograph a New York hustle to a song about celebrating and dressed the students in red, white, and blue. At one point the performers pulled out three large flags and began to dance with them. The audience cheered with incredible feeling every time they saw it. I cheered along with them. Whenever I introduced the number, I dedicated it to the lives that were lost. Students came closer to each other by dancing for something that was important to them.

Another favorite number that year was a takeoff of a popular movie. Misty was the choreographer, and we asked Valerie to be the star. She came out in a black and white, polka-dotted dress with a funny wig. Her lip-sync told of how evil she was while dancing around with eight men. The rest of the team entered doing a cha-cha that turned into a bouncy jive (fast swing). It ended with the boys carrying Valerie off over their heads.

Aside from the performing routines, camaraderie increased as a result of a yearly field trip. In January when I reminded my group of the upcoming Day of Dance, a new student raised his hand and questioned, "What's the Day of Dance?"

"Each year we take a bus to BYU-Idaho to have dance lessons for a day. They are taught by college teachers, students, and sometimes professionals," I explained. "You will see teenagers from many high schools. If you can come, meet in front of the school at 6:30 a.m. It is not mandatory, but I encourage participation to improve your dance technique."

It wasn't long before the day arrived and we drove the two and a half hours to Rexburg. In a large practice room, a male college student spoke up. "Welcome to our lift class here at BYU-Idaho. The first thing we want to point out is how important it is to be safe. Each couple should pair up with another couple to help spot. That means you catch them before they hit the floor." Fifty adolescents chuckled.

"Our first lift looks like this," said the instructor. His partner ran toward him, spun into a cradle position, and then flipped to land with her hips on his right shoulder. She was parallel to the floor with her arms out spread eagle.

"This is called the bird," he explained. And this is how you come out of it." The girl then fell forward diagonally to grab under his left arm into a flat lift as he turned her.

The group clapped. The demonstrators made it look easy. After the instructor explained some of the smaller details that would help them, he encouraged everyone to try it for themselves. The high school students immediately discovered it was not easy at all.

The first attempts were hilarious. Many girls were folded in half over the men's shoulders. Multiple tries went on in the same funny way. When they finally seemed to get the hang of it, more lifts were taught and more crazy attempts were made.

In the corner my light, 100-pound daughter Laura had paired off with Adam, a strong wrestler who executed each move like a pro. I noted how she looked at him with adoring eyes.

After awhile I went into another class to find Stephanie, my former student, doing an excellent job of teaching a swing. After class she excitedly revealed that she was a member of the BYUI Dance Team and had quickly become an instructor. She was going to tour a foreign country with them in the summer. I told her I was happy to see her continue her dream.

When I entered the foyer, a Preston couple with their arms linked exited the lift class and walked over to me. The girl exclaimed, "That class was the most fun ever! I loved the mambo lessons too."

The boy, however, rubbed his shoulder and said, "I think I'm going to feel this tomorrow. Did you see me, Alexis? I could do that one tough lift that hardly anyone got."

"Good job," I said. I talked to a few more keyed-up students, then, turned my head toward a noisy part of the room. I saw my daughter along with many other Preston students, lying on the floor with their heads on each other's stomachs playing the laughing game. Once someone giggled, jiggling a head, it started all the heads bobbing up and down on tummies. After chuckling for a while, I told the students to get their things, for it was time to go.

On the bus ride back to Preston, the teenagers played card games, sang songs, and I could hear their engaging conversations scattered with laughter.

My assistant, Misty, leaned over to me, "I think they had a good time, don't you?"

"Yes," I answered. Little did I realize then how those good times would bond them for life. My question now was, could I get my son Russell to become a ballroom dancer?

Patriotic number dedicated to those who died in 9/11

Valerie and her men

Day of Dance laughing game

Chapter 21

The Beat Goes On

Russell refused to dance as a freshman, wanting time to get used to high school. I was thrilled when he agreed to try out his sophomore year. He had the looks of his father with the same height and build. Stealing glances at Russ during my instruction, I was not overly surprised to see that he was a natural. The judges thought so too and picked him for the team.

During that year I had the Standard group do a medley of songs from the old movie, *Singing in the Rain*. The men did a section alone with umbrellas, and the girls shimmied to "All I Do Is Dream of You." At home after the first practice, Russell said, "I can't believe you are going to make us dance around with umbrellas."

I loved classic movies, especially MGM musicals, and played them often at home. My children knew more names of old actors than modern ones.

"Russell, haven't you ever wanted to be like Gene Kelly?" I questioned.

"The only Gene Kelly move I ever wanted to learn is the one where he falls onto his back and then whips himself up to a standing position."

I laughed. "Well, Russ, I would add that, except that I don't think the guys can do it. Gene Kelly was pretty buff." Russ immediately went into the living room, laid on the ground, and tried to flip to a standing position. His unsuccessful attempt made him look more like the comedian Donald O'Connor. When he at last made it upright, my other children and I yelled, "Bravo."

"Come to think of it," he added, "It would be cool to tap dance on roller skates."

Our *Singing in the Rain* number turned out wonderfully, but somehow I didn't think the students appreciated it as much as I did. I had worshipped Gene Kelly for years, but some of the teenagers had not even heard of him. Their homework assignment was to watch the classic movie.

Although my son was a good dancer, Russ had a mind of his own. Sometimes during class he refused to hold out an arm like I told him, or he would make up his own pose, finding pleasure in annoying me. Nonetheless, I observed that although Russ did not act like he was listening, he tried to apply the technique I taught, which resulted in him looking very good on the dance floor.

It was obvious to me that the girls were attracted to him, for when he passed them, the women would stare and sigh. His oblivion made it seem even more comical. He already had many friends and was very popular at school, but dancing gave Russell an edge.

My daughter Laura kept me clued in on his activities. "Mom, you should see Russ at the school dances doing the cha-cha, the waltz, and the swing with other ballroom girls. I can't believe it. He puts on the air that he is too cool for ballroom, and yet he is better at it than anyone."

Laura was gaining much from ballroom long before we began to see it in Russell. Choreographing two dances was Laura's plan for her senior project, a polka for the B team and an adagio number. After her first practice with the backup team, she said, "Mom, they can't even figure out how to do a basic polka turn. We repeated it over and over again, but I don't know if they will ever get it."

"Remember they are beginners, Laura. Over the next few months you will be surprised how much they will improve. I think you are learning a little of the challenge of teaching."

"You're right, Mom. This is harder than I thought."

Her number turned out to be creative with many changing formations and fun lifts, bringing out the best in her students and rhythmic clapping from the audiences.

Meanwhile, Laura worked hard on her adagio in the early morning with Adam as her partner and two other couples. Laura and Adam had learned the one-hand lift at the Day of Dance and used it in the routine, even though no one else could do it. Adam had won first place at the State Wrestling Meet in his weight category that year. Strength for the lift was important, but the key was also timing and the girl knowing how to balance herself, arching her back, and tightening her muscles at just the right moment.

The lift involved Laura running to Adam with a jump, while he hoisted her holding her hips to balance over his head. She looked like an airplane with her arms out. As he flipped her sideways, she placed a hand on his shoulder while he let go with the other hand. It was spine chilling to watch as she posed with her lower leg bent and the free arm extended.

Laura's thoughtful choreography to the beautiful music, along with everyone's impeccable synchronization made it one of the best lift numbers yet. The skill of teaching she acquired would be used again and again.

Laura's group of dancing buddies could be real clowns sometimes. With my birthday on April Fools' Day, you would think I'd be ready for anything, but nothing equaled what happened when I walked into ballroom practice that day, in Laura's senior year.

On the floor were two large boxes printed with the words Maytag. Loudly I asked, "Hey, did you guys get me a washer and dryer for my birthday?" Suddenly, out popped three or four impish boys from each box. Wearing nothing but jean cutoffs and bow ties, they ran to a line and began to do the Charleston from our all-girl section in "Singing in the Rain" — "All I do is Dream of You." My sides became sore with laughter as they bounced around. They ended with a boisterous, "Happy Birthday, Alexis!" I was embarrassed but touched that they would go to all the trouble to do a unique dance just for me.

Laura's ballroom friends meant a lot to her. She described her feelings in an essay she wrote for the Idaho State Writing Test. She had to choose a hobby, class, or activity and show how it was beneficial to her and to others:

The music starts. I'm sitting by the wall, my hands fidgeting in my lap with the words, 'I can't take this anymore!' going through my mind. I stand up and begin the slow, hard walk to the other side of the gym, my heart skipping. All of a sudden I see him. Our eyes lock and I almost melt as I utter the simple phrase, 'Wanna dance?'

With a simple 'yes' he offers me his arm and escorts me onto the dance floor. In perfect dance position, we waltz around the room, and I feel as though I'm Lois Lane holding the hand of Superman. We fly across the dance floor. The music stops. Our flight ends as he escorts me off the dance floor with a humble 'Thank you.' I may be sitting by the wall again, but inside I'm still soaring.

Ballroom dance is the expression of emotions through motion. From the polka to the tango, it is my most favorite thing to do in the whole world. If I had to choose between ballroom dance and playing the piano or violin, running cross-country, and everything else that I do, I would choose ballroom dance any day!

"Ballroom dance has been very beneficial to me. I've grown stronger physically, socially, and maybe even mentally from dancing. For some it's a really hard thing to ask someone to dance, but ballroom has given me courage to just go for it and ask the guy. Practicing three times a week with my dance team has made me strong. And socially, I just let go at dances and I have a ball!

I've seen and heard how dancing has affected others. My partner's mother told me that being on the dance team was such a good thing for her son. His grades were getting better, and he seemed to be more happy and upbeat. I've seen the freshmen that make the team come in all shy and quiet, but by the end of the first month you wouldn't know them!

They say the best things in life are your friends, and I would have to say that is the best thing about ballroom. I've made so many good friends. Ballroom is just the best way to relax, be yourself, and have fun!

After I read Laura's paper, I knew she recognized the same things that I did about this activity. She was one of those shy freshmen, herself, who found confidence. I rejoiced that she had made so many special friends.

Adam and Laura in the one arm lift

Alexis' birthday surprise

A special birthday dance

Chapter 22

Always Do Your Best

A hundred teenagers were talking with excitement as they waited for tryouts to start in the gym. I noticed Ted sitting over by the wall alone. I could not believe he was here after I kicked him off the team a year ago for poor attendance and intolerable tardiness. He was a great dancer and I hated losing him.

I walked over to him and said, "If I put you on the team this year, Ted, you have to have better attendance. You can't be late. When the school play is on, you can't miss ballroom." Ted, with his great voice, always ended up in the high school musical.

"I will do better this year, Mrs. Beckstead. You can count on it."

"I'll give you another chance if you're sincere about that."

Ted aced the tryout like I thought he would, and I put him back on the team hoping he had learned his lesson.

The second semester came and the school musical practices began. Over half of my ballroom members were involved. As Mr. Saunders put it, "Students who sing are also students who dance." I appreciated the fact that Mr. Saunders held his play practices after school, so they would not conflict with ballroom. However, some of the participants kept missing my class as it got closer to the play performances, because they stayed up late trying to fit everything into their lives.

But it was different with Ted. Ted had fine attendance all year and was never tardy. Though he had a main role in the play, he was determined to be dedicated to the dance team like he promised. That impressed me. Mr. Saunders had a few late practices, but there was Ted every morning at 6:50 a.m. never missing once during the play season.

I couldn't keep it in any longer. "Ted, you have set some high goals for yourself this year. I am so proud of you for being able to achieve them. You have learned one of the most important things that will make you happy in life—being dependable. I think you are the greatest." He smiled, glad to know his efforts had not gone unnoticed.

For years after, I told Ted's story to ballroom students explaining that they could achieve whatever goal they wanted if they were committed to it.

After he graduated, Ted danced on the Utah State team and worked hard at a job that helped him get a degree. Later I heard he had become a successful business manager.

Rachael was another success story. She was always late. I reminded her often that she needed to do better. But for three years I could always expect to see her walk in ten minutes past the hour. Sometimes her dawdling held up entrance cues. I put up with it solely because she was an incredible dancer and I hated to lose her.

Then one day when she was a senior, it dawned on me that she was always early. I said, "Rachael, what has happened to you? You are on time now. How come?"

"I'm glad you noticed," she said. "I was tired of everyone being mad at me. I woke up one morning and said to myself, I am not going to be a late anymore."

"Wow! I can't believe it, Rachael. I am so happy about that."

"You know what? I am happier too," she admitted. "It didn't feel good to let people down, so I am not going to do it anymore."

Later I found out the rest of the story. She eventually confided that it wasn't only a matter of making up her mind. She needed help and she knew it. Being attracted to a punctual boy on the team, she figured out how to kill two birds with one stone. She could spend more time with the early bird, if she could get him to pick her up in the morning. The motivation just might shift her into a hurry-up flight pattern. She didn't want him sitting out in the car waiting for her. So that's how Rachael cured her lateness problem and started a relationship with a boy who would come to mean a great deal to her.

I wish that I could say all my students learned the lesson Ted and Rachael did, but it was not always the case. Most years I kicked someone off the team for poor attendance or tardiness.

We had an experience where a whole team had to learn a lesson the hard way. After my daughter Laura taught her polka number to the B team, the time came for them to perform at a basketball half time. At our warm-up before the game, I explained to the students that I expected them to be ready in costumes, in the northwest entrance three minutes before the end of the second quarter.

The appointed time came. I went to the northwest doors, and there were no B-team members. I immediately ran around trying to find a sign of them, checking locker rooms and bathrooms, not finding anyone. When Laura appeared, I told her to help with the search or we were going to be terribly embarrassed at the 500 people left wondering where the entertainment was. By this time I was a nervous wreck and began pacing back and forth. The clock ticked on. Suddenly, thirty seconds before the group needed to make an entrance, they all came running down the hall to line up.

Laura came behind panting, "I found them on the other side of the school in a bathroom. They lost track of the time," she reported.

The B team made their entrance and the number was well received. But I felt betrayed. At the next practice, I let the students know they couldn't have the privilege of performing if they were not more responsible.

They felt bad to have let me down, so they gave me a signed card expressing remorse and recommitment. I was glad they wanted to do better.

I thought this could be a teaching situation for the A team as well, so I spoke to them about what happened.

"I want you all to understand that the most important thing you learn in ballroom is not dancing. It is being responsible and on time when you say you will. If you learn that, you will be successful your whole life. Be a person of integrity; it is what I want you to learn most in ballroom dance."

The B team was never late again for a performance that year. But because new people joined the team each fall, dependability had to be taught continually. A typical performance often went something like this: Before a show, one girl would tell me she lost her shoes and forgot to bring her nylons. Another girl would say she couldn't find her black skirt. Two students never showed up.

In the end, the girl without shoes borrowed a pair from a friend (which were two sizes too big), the other girl wore a skirt from home that did not match, and the two students without partners danced together very awkwardly because they weren't used to each other. Thereafter, the first girl kept better track of her shoes and stockings. The girl with the lost skirt found it and was more careful to keep her costumes together. The students who didn't show up were reprimanded by their peers, and were more mindful of dancing commitments.

At other performances the same theatrics would repeat themselves, but with different lost items and different teenagers. Some learned a lesson; others did not. Throughout my dancing years, my headaches continued because of the large number of youth I worked with and the multitude of costume pieces involved. Sometimes it would send me to practices pleading with them to take charge of their lives, so I could be relieved of the burden. They would do better for a while, but it never stopped completely.

All these incidents, I decided, are part of the step-by-step process each individual has to go through before they make up their mind to take responsibility. Ballroom dancing created opportunities for the students to learn these important lessons.

There were other things to be learned as well. I walked in the house one night to hear my husband ask, "How did the basketball halftime performance go tonight?"

"Alright, I guess."

"Only alright?" he questioned. "You know, you ought to quit performing at basketball games. It lowers ballroom dancing."

"I beg to differ. I think ballroom dancing gives class to basketball games. I admit, though, that I am frustrated. I know my students can do better. They are not giving me all they've got. Do you have any suggestions on how I can get them to try harder?"

"Maybe you should scream and yell like the sports coaches," he replied.

I shook my head. "That's just not me. I can't bring myself to do that."

David said, "You need to remember you are working with teenagers."

What he said was true. Sometimes teenagers seemed to care more about fun than perfection. But I knew there was more for them to give. I sat on the couch and ruminated all evening on how I could affect these young people, recalling the idealistic conversation David and I had in college years ago. "The best way for people to change and improve is from within. The best way to lead is with love."

How could I get them to have a desire to be their best?

The next morning at practice I resolved to do what all sports coaches do—give a pep talk.

After the students had gathered and quieted down, I said, "I want to tell you what has been on my mind. The performance went okay last night, but I don't want 'okay.' I think you can do better than that. Someone gave me the suggestion that I scream and yell at you." Many shook their heads in distaste.

I continued, "What I'd rather have is for each of you to find the desire within your own heart to give your all. If you learn to do your best in everything you undertake now, then you will be successful and happy in your life. You'll have people's respect. Family and employers will value and appreciate you."

"Some of you take great pride in marching to your own beat, in doing things your own way. I can understand that. But if, while you are here, you will learn to be 'one' with each other by doing the steps and moves the same way and dancing as a team and not as an individual, separate from others, then you will experience the beauty of perfect unity—a kinship and bond with everyone in this room. It would be a great accomplishment. Audiences would be in awe of your unity."

"It is imperative that each of you make the goal to practice with all your might, to perform with all you've got, and strive to become a truly unified team."

"There may be times when you feel you don't have the ability to be a great dancer. That's when you need to turn to God and ask him to help you. The only reason I've been able to do all the choreography and carry the load of this program is because I have sought help from the Lord. He will help you, too, if you go to him."

Their eyes brightened. Enlightened determination moved across their faces like the dawning of a new day. Our practice that morning, and for weeks to come, was outstanding. The teenagers had taken my suggestion and applied it in their lives. My heart felt like a rejoicing choir on Easter morning.

The next month the dancers saw the payoff when the Latin team won first place in their division at the Gem State Dance Competition for an impeccable performance of a combined funk and New York hustle dance that was full of energy. They gave it their best, and we were overjoyed at the outcome.

At our closing concert that spring, after our finale number, my students gave me flowers and a gift. The present was a beautiful picture of a path and door with the words, "I am the Way, the Truth, and the Life." The attached note, signed by all the dancers said, "Thanks for not only coordinating our feet, but putting us on His path to success." Witnessing my students learn important lessons that would make them happy, was my greatest reward.

One young man needed no lessons in devotion. James proved himself stalwart when he drove into practice one morning. The car stalled on the side of the road, but not wanting to miss dance class, he ran six miles into town without stopping and made it on time. He rehearsed the full hour like he wasn't even tired, proving that some people will go to any lengths to ballroom dance.

Preston High Team, first place at the Gem State Competition in their division

Chapter 23

A Little Convincing

Having the support of many people was essential to the success of my ballroom program. When Misty was not able to teach for me any longer, Sherri Rallison, the mother of one of my students, volunteered to assist me. She did not have technical ballroom training, but there was no one else who could help. Sherri was an enthusiastic partner in the cause and handled our music editing. There were many other important people behind the scenes, such as, my husband helping with my children when I was gone, administrators providing practice space and performance opportunities, secretaries helping with the handling of money, school sound people running music, janitors setting up and cleaning rooms, and parental supervision. I was grateful for everyone's help and especially their willingness.

Unfortunately, not all were so willing. Some needed a little convincing. The elementary school principal was very kind to let us use the gym and cafeteria at his building. He knew there was no room at the high school for us to practice. When he retired, a new principal was hired who was hesitant to have my dancers use his facilities. Although he gave reluctant permission at first, partway through the year he told me that he wanted us out of the cafeteria and suggested we move to a less-convenient, multipurpose room. I got vibes that he would like to get rid of us altogether. We cooperated, though, and switched our practice to the other room.

Later that year when I called the principal to coordinate a ballroom dance assembly for his students, he wanted to change our regular arrangements. I tried to be patient and work with his suggestions. That effort paid off.

We did some unique numbers for the assembly, one being a spine-tingling paso doble to a particularly exciting piece of music. The men were dressed like pirates with scarves around their heads, purple sashes, and an earring in one ear with the girls in purple, ruffled dresses. The choreography was a challenge for me, but the dramatic music let my imagination run wild as I made up moves to fit the pulsing beat.

At one point everyone backed into a half circle, while two pirates ran to do handstands on the shoulders of kneeling men, flipping in the air to land on their feet. As they moved over, two other pirates ran forward holding a girl above them, then, slid her across the floor. More men set her to arch over the shoulder of her partner, and he spun her dizzily. Behind, everyone else moved to a pyramid shape and began flipping the women left and right as though they were capes. Turning away from their partners, the girls rolled to an ending lung pose as the music abruptly stopped. The faces of the children appeared stunned as they let out a big "Wow!"

The children were also impressed with our lift routine. Because of their strength, I had asked three wrestlers to be a part of it. I thought they could easily do the T-press. But at practice, two of them did it easily, while one boy struggled, not quite able to lock his arms. After his continued failure I told them that we could take the T-press out and do something else. The boy having difficulties would not hear of it. He was determined and kept at it over the next month. His friends never gave him a bad time and only encouraged him. The day he was able to lock his arms, the other boys gave him triumphant high fives. At the elementary school assembly, the children oohed and aahed at each lift, especially the T-press.

The new principal asked the children to applaud for us again at the end of the show and thanked us for coming. Later he approached me, "Mrs. Beckstead, I must admit that I was skeptical about your teenagers practicing here at my elementary school. I worried about them interacting with the little children, not knowing if it would be a good thing. But you work with wonderful students, and I now think they are a good influence on the elementary age kids. It is clear the children look up to and admire them. I am very glad you are teaching here at my school. The assembly was wonderful. The teachers said it is something they look forward to every year more than any other event. If there is anything I can do to help you, please let me know."

We had another convert to ballroom dance. A couple of days later I received many thank you cards from the second grade classes. There were adorable crayon drawings of boys lifting girls over their heads. One child wrote, "I want to be a ballroom dancer."

Similarly, our junior high principal left and a new administrator was hired named Mrs. Call.

I had heard about her strictness before I phoned to set up an assembly at the school. Explaining to her that we usually did two performances to accommodate the sixth, seventh, and eighth graders, Mrs. Call immediately responded that she only wanted one performance for the seventh and eighth grade classes and wouldn't let the sixth graders come. I tried to talk her out of her decision, but she would not hear of it.

A day later, Mrs. Call contacted me and humbly offered, "The sixth grade teachers were terribly upset about being left out of the assembly. They made a big fuss, claiming that this was the one assembly they looked forward to all year and wanted their students to be included. So, let's add the extra performance."

Wanting to laugh out loud, I restrained myself and told her we would do the show twice. After the assemblies, Mrs. Call was hooked. She never gave us any more trouble and was thereafter very accommodating and full of praise.

When Al Koch retired as principal of the high school, I worried about the new replacement. What if the new principal was not supportive like Al? Directors from other school districts had shared with me their frustrations about their administrators not giving them financial help or performance time for their dance teams. I didn't want those troubles in Preston.

At the beginning of the year, I had a chance to meet the new principal when I was at the school office. Dr. Betty Tanner, a middle-aged brunette, stepped forward confidently and said, "So you are Mrs. Beckstead. I've heard so much about you and your dance program. It sounds terrific. Do you mind if I stop by to see your tryouts tomorrow morning?"

Her pleasant attitude made me feel less apprehensive.

"No, not at all," I answered. I told her the time and place. As I prepared to leave, I said, "It is very nice to meet you. Good luck with your new assignment."

The next morning when I was counting out steps in a large gym, Dr. Tanner walked in with a look of surprise at the hundred teenagers dancing the cha-cha to engaging music. A smile formed on her face and she watched for a long time.

Halfway through the practice I told the teens to take a few minutes to get a drink. I approached Dr. Tanner, and she began, "Alexis, this is incredible. I can't believe you can get all these students here before school to do this. It is great to see them having such a good time."

"When I first started," I began to explain, "I used to have them dance only a few steps. Then I decided to teach them two routines, so they could have more fun."

"Well, I'm impressed, I must say," the principal commented. "You can expect my full support."

"Thanks for coming," I told her. Turning to the students now trailing in, I said. "Okay, everyone line up. I have a limerick for you." A student named Tim was on mind when I wrote it.

He had grace, charm and suave not by chance.
His charisma could not be enhanced.
Where did he find
This high class divine?
My dear, he took up Ballroom Dance.

The students laughed and I went on with the teaching.

Betty tried to come to as many of our performances as she could during the school year. Near the end of her first year as principal, Dr. Tanner told me, "Alexis, your program is my favorite of all the activities we offer here at the school. I've decided to give you more club money next year to help with costumes." She couldn't have told me anything that I wanted more to hear. I knew first hand that having a supportive principal made all the difference.

During the years we performed at varsity basketball halftimes, I was aware that the coach never saw us dance at these games because he spent all the half times in the locker room encouraging his team. Taking on the part-time position of athletic director after he retired from coaching, Mr. Pratt still continued to go to the basketball games, but now he was able to see our entertainment.

After the first game of the season, he came up to me and said, "Alexis, I can't believe it. They are fantastic! This is such a great thing you are doing. Let's see if we can get you more performances. Why don't we have you perform at the junior varsity games also?"

I thanked him. His suggestion would now give our backup team more opportunities.

The cooperative spirit of all the fine people in Preston is what really made ballroom dancing so powerful in our small town. Observing the enthusiastic teens perform was all the convincing needed to gain support.

Pirate number

Second grade thank you cards.

Chapter 24

The Best Policy

One day a writer for a popular magazine based in New York called me up and asked questions about my high school ballroom dance program. A college director had given her my name. After conversing with her for awhile, I figured out that she was not really interested in my team but wanted to write an article to show that popular ballroom shows on TV were increasing dancing all over the country.

"Our community was well entrenched in ballroom dancing," I told her, "long before the TV shows came on because of the high school team. Maybe it's true that Hollywood has made ballroom dancing more acceptable now, but I have been disappointed that in some instances they make ballroom dancing look like a sex show. Here in Preston, Idaho we try to keep it the wholesome activity it can be by having our students wear modest costumes and avoid suggestive moves. Ballroom dancing can be classy and uplifting. It doesn't have to be seedy or low-minded."

She said she found my comments interesting, but I never heard from her again.

Later I read in a dance history book that Aristotle considered dance to be an important means of moral training and to be useful in helping to purge a youth's soul of undesirable emotions (*History of the Dance in Art and Education*, by Richard Kraus, Sarah Hilsendager, Brenda Dixon, Prentice-Hall, 1991, p. 44). I asked myself, *How can that take place if the teens are only half dressed and move seductively?*

One evening I discovered how my students felt about costuming. At a varsity basketball game one night, I went to check on my performers in the hall and announced, "Now you understand that a visiting jazz group is going to dance first. The minute they are finished, you go ahead and walk on."

The Latin team members nodded their heads. At that moment the girls in the jazz group sauntered past us dressed in tight, low-necked, backless costumes that were very revealing.

One of my Latin girls leaned over to me and whispered, "I'm glad you don't make us dress like that."

The comment took me back. Living in a conservative, religious community, I didn't think the students' parents would like their teenagers dressing skimpy, and I knew I didn't want my daughters in such clothes. So I always tried to keep the costumes modest. But it was nice to discover the youth appreciated costumes that covered them. In fact, the girls often asked if they could wear shorts under their dresses.

One performance revealed that the community appreciated modesty as well. In December our group performed at the hospital bazaar, which was set up at the high school gym. The dance floor was surrounded by old-fashioned booths selling food and gifts. After we danced, a college team performed several ballroom numbers. Before class at our next practice one of the students spoke up, "I had all kinds of people tell me that they liked our high school team better than the college team at the bazaar.

"I heard the same thing," added someone else.

Sharing my observations, I said, "The college team was actually better than our team. They had excellent technique, but the problem was that they were dressed in very revealing costumes. That immediately made everyone in the audience uncomfortable and actually embarrassed. Our team, being fully clothed, was more fun to watch because the audience could relax and enjoy all the motion without dwelling on the scantiness of clothing. Why don't people figure that out?" Those who heard my comments nodded their agreement.

We received more feedback at a February competition. Some parents who came to watch the program told us. "We just want you to know that we love your dance group. We especially look for them every year when we come here, because we know you will always have creative, fun numbers. Your kids are so wholesome and full of energy. They don't do suggestive movements or wear vulgar costumes. They just have a great time. Even if your teams don't win the competition every time, we want you to know that Preston is our favorite group to watch."

We were surprised. Sherri and I did not realize how much Preston students stood out. One of the main coordinators of the competition and her assistant gave us similar comments.

My own personal feelings are that ballroom dancing should raise people, not lower them.

That takes place through what they wear and how they move.

A popular news magazine once described teenagers and the challenges in dealing with them. It said teens have two very distinct influences in their lives — one is an intense physical attraction for the opposite sex and the other is an amazing amount of energy and aggression. Parents often struggle to keep their teens under control in these areas so they do not get out of hand.

I feel ballroom dancing is a positive way to use these characteristics appropriately so that adolescents can have a sense of fulfillment rather than frustration. Through dancing, teenagers can have the pleasure of being near the opposite sex in an acceptable way while using their astounding energy to create a work of art. At the same time they are developing a sense of belonging with their peers. If we dress them inappropriately and teach them to dance suggestively, we are not helping them learn proper behavior at all and only creating more problems. When it comes to costuming, modesty is the best policy.

Chapter 25

Danceoholics

Often students came along who caught the dance bug in an intense way and took their love to great heights. Not satisfied learning three team numbers each year, they pleaded to do specialties and sometimes asked if they could choreograph their own dances. They volunteered to teach the backup team, got involved in community dance events, and took the initiative as leaders to provide dance opportunities for others.

At one early practice three tall senior boys walked toward me with anxious looks. Jacob, the obvious leader of the group, a good-looking boy with spiked hair, spoke up, "Alexis, we want to make up a three-couple, Lindy hop specialty by ourselves. We will pick our own partners and come up with our own costumes. Is that okay with you?"

"Sure," I said. They immediately gave each other high fives.

"Hey Dude, it's going to be great," Jacob told his friends confidently.

"Do you have some music?" I asked.

"Yeah, it is right here," answered Jake. "I'll play it for you after class."

Later Jake played his song, a dynamic, lively tune with lots of ripples and jump sounds. The name "Lindy" is short for Lindberg, the first man to fly across the Atlantic Ocean. The Lindy hop gives the appearance of flying through space with arms, sometimes stretching out like airplane wings.

For a month and a half Jake and his friends came in at 6:30 a.m. to practice before class, impressing me with their motivation. Their dance turned out exceptionally, so I set up a basketball halftime performance. I had not seen their costumes beforehand. It was quite a sight when the boys walked out in long Zoot suits.

"Ooh!" went the audience. Their number was full of lifts, 40's-style kick steps and flying Lindy moves. The boys hammed it up by pretending to comb their hair and straighten their lapels, while the girls fought between each other over the men. The gentlemen separated the women by throwing their partners over their shoulders. The dance was a hit, a glory moment for their senior year giving them the opportunity to work cooperatively, organize, and use their creativity.

There were many students like them that just couldn't get enough. Danceoholics volunteered constantly to leap into any routine where people were missing with no apprehension about learning on demand. Occasionally the Student Exec Council called an assembly practice during our regular class time and left us with poor attendance, but sometimes those were the best practices we had—where dance lovers jumped into unknown spots to adlib, providing a comedy.

Two such danceoholics were Tim and Kristina. They were Standard dancers with natural ability, but every time I turned around, they were learning the Latin dances to be helpful or just for fun. When a couple in our superhero medley had conflicts with some of the performances, Tim and Kristina spent extra hours learning the new dance, getting a kick out of wearing the black masks and leather gloves that were part of the costumes.

A dance I always wanted to choreograph was the quickstep, but knowing how hard it is for long-legged people to keep up the fast pace, I never attempted to teach it until Tim and Kristina were seniors.

With them in mind for this solo, I found a song that was playful, lively, and infectious. I couldn't believe how easily they picked up the first round of running, gliding maneuvers that took them across the floor. I added jumps and slides to fit the music and then taught them Gold steps like the six-quick twinkle and running finish. At this point when the music changed, I had Tim scoop Kristina onto his shoulder to sit backwards where he could lift her straight over his head by one leg and one arm. The words in the song rang out loudly, "That's more like it!" Tim turned her, dropped her into a catch position, and twirled her to a cute ending pose. The couple loved dancing it.

After high school, Kristina taught dancing whenever she could and Tim continued his ballroom training in college, increasing his skills to a point I never expected.

One summer I had the opportunity to invite a professional to teach a slow waltz solo to a special couple who were very dedicated to my program. Armando, tall, well-built, and likeable, was one of the most handsome boys to ever be part of my group. Paige was a stunning blond with a radiant smile and attractive figure. Andrea Hales, had assisted on "Dancing with the Stars," a popular TV dance show, and that alone made my students very nervous.

Andrea not only choreographed a lovely dance for them, but was not content until they did it with perfect technique. I chuckled at Armando's red face as Andrea manipulated his body to conform to her shapely physique. Not used to such familiar maneuvers, he caught on quickly to avoid further jerking of his torso. I tell you, after his four-day encounter with Andrea, his topline was gorgeous ever after.

Paige struggled at first, but Andrea was able to bring out grace in her as never before seen. With Paige in a new, lavender ballroom gown and Armando in tails, the final creation came together. Performing again and again over the next few months, the self-confidence of the couple soared. I especially could not get over the change in Paige. She seemed to turn into a butterfly overnight.

I overheard girls on my team whisper about how gorgeous Armando was. One day after watching him run through his romantic solo, Leanne could not hold it in any longer and shouted, "Armando, I am going to marry you, okay?"

At the conclusion of my spring concert a year later, Paige was flying around the room during general dancing. She had refined her movements even more, gaining a real classy flare. When I had the chance to talk to her, she excitedly told me of the dance classes she had taken at Brigham Young University in Provo and how she had made the ballroom dance team at my alma mater.

Months later, I witnessed her perform an advanced quickstep with the refined college group, a glorious moment for both of us. Because of the stiff competition to make the BYU team in Provo, it was especially rewarding. Afterwards I threw my arms around her rejoicing in her accomplishment. I knew the fun that was in store for her.

Another danceoholic was Whitney. I attended her senior presentation, and the first thing she said was, "Dancing is a passion with me! That's why I decided to do my project around it."

Smiling, I thought of how true it was—this girl absolutely loved to dance! She had been on the Latin team for four years, often came in early to help others, taught the B team a number, did many specialties, and made up her own dances. She could not get enough.

Whitney continued to describe the dance competition she organized, doing all the planning herself—scheduling a building, hanging up flyers in surrounding schools, arranging judges, awards, and music people. She expressed her dismay at all that went on behind the scenes to make such a production come about. She mentioned her chagrin when some individuals didn't follow through, which gave her more work. I laughed inside thinking of all the headaches I had endured over the years running my program. She was beginning to understand what it was like.

Mentally, I remembered the day of her competition and the great turnout. Whitney included a category in which couples had to make up their own ballroom routine. Many B-team couples stretched and improved themselves, dancing better than I had ever seen them before. The whole thing was a success.

Pondering on the timid Whitney I had known when she was a freshman, it was hard to believe that this was the same person. Dancing had changed her life. Doing her senior project around this sport had given her a chance to develop leadership. Dancing was something she couldn't leave alone. It was the love of her life. And I knew just how she felt.

At our ballroom practices, Sherri's son, Stephen, was an agile standout. His remarkable talent put him on the Latin team in his freshman year. Not being satisfied, he wanted to take private lessons from professionals to compete. Meanwhile, his cousin, who lived in Nevada, had the same feelings. She and Stephen became long-distance partners. Steve flew to Nevada once in awhile, and she came up to Preston so they could take lessons and practice together.

In Steve's junior year a performing group cancelled their exhibition for a varsity basketball halftime. Steve's cousin happened to be in town, so we asked them to do a solo at the last minute. I knew Steve was gifted. But when he danced with his cousin, a girl with incredible skill, Steve was able to fly. The audience loved them.

During that year he taught a swing to the B team and choreographed a specialty mambo. He worked well with the students and his numbers were creative. Watching Steve practice one day, I noticed how his dance partners seemed to come alive and step up to his level. He brought out the best in his companions.

At the closing concert Steve and his cousin danced a solo that was a hit with the audience. It was also no surprise to me that they won over the college students at the competitions that year. Sherri was tickled to see her son become a ballroom star.

The word got out that they were having tryouts for the movie *High School Musical 3* in Salt Lake City because of all the dance ability in the area. Steve went down to see how he could do. When he arrived, he found he was competing with many professionals. However, out of about 900 dancers, Steve made the cut for the top thirty.

The director complimented Stephen and said that unlike those who danced with precision because of experience, he recognized Steve as a talented teen who danced for the sheer joy of it. He said he kept Steve around to inspire the others. Although he did not make the final cut, the tryout did a lot for Stephen's self-esteem. He continued to win competitions through his senior year, taught classes for his mother's studio, and danced in college. I knew he would kick up his heels for life.

One January at the Day of Dance, a tall gentleman with a familiar face brought a youth group for instruction. I knew him from my BYU days but could not remember his name. I had to find out. Walking up to him I said, "You were on the Social Dance Team at BYU in 1978, weren't you?"

He nodded and stated, "You were on the Standard Team at BYU when I was there."

"You're right," I commented. "We went on the Northern California Tour together."

He agreed and introduced himself as Bob Frost. "You married your dance partner, David Beckstead."

"I did." I told him of our moving to Preston with David setting up his medical practice there. Bob said that aside from his regular job, he taught dancing to a group in Boise and brought them here for lessons. He introduced his wife and pointed out his son and daughter who were in a class as well. Later I introduced them to my children, Laura and Russell.

I told Bob, "You know, when I was on the Standard team in college, we were always jealous of the Social Dance Team, since we thought you were much better dancers than we were."

"That's funny," he said. "The Social Team thought International Style was the ultimate dance form, and we were jealous of you." We both laughed. I marveled at how people like Bob and I could not get dancing out of our blood.

We were not content unless we were passing on the joy to our children and others. All the high school teams of Idaho and Utah had been started by BYU ballroom team alumni. Dancing wasn't something you could keep to yourself. Many of my students felt the same way and went on to share the "passion."

Armando Crosland and Paige Christensen, Waltz Solo

Ryan Hemsley and Paige Christensen, members
of the BYU Ballroom Dance Company

PART III
The Influence of Dance

"Life, at no matter what age,
can be full and exciting!"

Buzz Champneys

Chapter 26

Effect on the Community

The Preston High Ballroom program touched the lives of many in the community, its impact being very powerful on one family in particular.

My husband came home for lunch one afternoon with some shocking news. "You remember Tom and Joanna Steiner who have been on your team?"

"Yes." Tom, a member of my first team, was a bright spot who added laughs to every practice. Lovely Joanna was still in my group. I remembered the wild swing she did with my son, Dave.

"Their father just passed away. He wasn't very old—middle aged," reported my doctor husband.

"David, that is so sad."

When I expressed my sympathy to Joanna in class, she remarked, "It is a hard thing to go through, but my father was so miserable that it is nice to know he isn't suffering anymore. Don't worry. We are going to be fine."

About a year later when I asked Joanna how her mother was doing, she said, "Instead of watching our Mom sit around feeling sorry for herself, Tom and I talked her into going to a church dance. You know what a good leader Tom is. He made our mother dance with him, and he taught her some steps. Mom had so much fun that she started going to the Adult Singles dances where she met a really nice man. They are going to get married. Because you taught us to love dancing, we wanted our mother to love it too. And now she is marrying a man who enjoys it as well."

I suddenly recalled that my grandparents had met at a church dance, and responded with, "You just never know how things will turn out, do you?"

Dancing had changed the whole future and happiness of this family. At that time, we had no idea the fulfillment it would give to Joanna.

Our group added much to community productions and events of all kinds in the area, the interest in ballroom dancing increasing from year to year. Parents often called asking how they could prepare their children for my team, or to ask if I offered an adult dancing class. I could only do so much and did not have time for more teaching, but something happened to fill the demand.

Autumn was one of my first students, a talented and enthusiastic dancer, who learned a cha-cha solo her senior year. After high school she went to BYU-Idaho and made the college team. She married, moved back to our area, and started a dance studio in Preston, teaching clogging and ballroom dancing to young children. Her classes were so popular they filled immediately with a waiting list. When I saw Autumn's groups perform at different events around town, I was astonished at how well they did for such a young age. Because of her program, freshmen were now trying out with more experience, increasing the quality of my teams. Autumn also started an adult ballroom class, causing more people to dance than ever before.

A few years later Autumn called me on the phone. "Alexis, you know that I live over here on the west side of the valley. I am seriously thinking of starting a ballroom team at the West Side High. I'd sure like them to have a team like Preston High. I am a little nervous about it, though. Would you tell me how you run your program?"

I was excited about her desire and began a huge sales pitch on the idea. "Oh Autumn, you would be making so many people happy. I'd love to see that happen."

I told her about the tryouts we had, the times we met, where I got dance shoes, and the fees I collected from the students, encouraging her in every possible way to make a go of it.

As it turned out, Autumn had the motivation and leadership qualities to make it happen. At a school of only 125 students, she was able to get together a nice size group. With her college training behind her, she choreographed some clever numbers.

Every spring my team put on an assembly for the West Side elementary and junior high schools. We now included Autumn's group in the performance, starting a new tradition. I was elated to see the happy West Siders join the fun.

Other opportunities arose for my students to teach in the community. Kristina wanted to do a unique senior project that had never been attempted. Her idea was to organize a mini ballroom dance camp for children and teens. After requesting me to be her mentor, she explained her plans.

"Well, I am going to invite about fifty individuals between the ages of ten and eighteen to come to a three-day camp with classes in cha-cha, waltz, and swing. We will have it after school. Saturday night we will have the participants perform what they have learned for their families and friends. I would like to have the high school team perform several numbers that night, too. I am not opening it up to everyone, so I don't end up with hundreds of people and get in over my head. As you know, ballroom dance is very popular in our town."

I nodded my agreement.

She continued, "I will choreograph the routines and ask some of the team members to help me teach."

"Fabulous, Kristina. Do you mind if my eleven-year-old daughter, Karrie, comes?"

"I'd love to have her."

Later my son, Russell, told me that Kristina had invited him to come to the camp, as well. Russ always dragged his feet in my ballroom practices. I did not expect him to be interested in the camp. But just like my older son, Wes, if a girl asked him, then it was a whole different matter.

When Kristina's camp started, the younger children looked darling all paired up.

Peeking into Russell's class, I saw a side to him I had never seen before. Wanting to impress the girls, he did the cha-cha like a pro. Not only did he show incredible styling with the proper shifting of weight, but he threw in silly facial expressions and head turns raising his eyebrows—what a comedian. He was a one-man show, making everyone around him laugh. It was Donald O'Connor all over again.

Kristina decided to throw in a lift class and the older couples were soon involved using all their strength. Kristina addressed the group, "You might think that the man does all the work in lifts, but that is wrong. A girl has to work just as hard. She needs to tighten every muscle and push or pull with all her might. It is really hard for a man to lift a floppy girl, no matter how light she is."

Russell was in his territory. He enjoyed twirling his partner through the air showing off his biceps. Besides watching my son have fun, it was good to see many inexperienced teenagers discovering their wings.

Parents and family members were in attendance at the ending show, clapping at their children's performances. The camp was a giant success. Many of the attendees later tried out for the high school team and made it, all due to Kristina's dance camp.

After our regular rehearsal one day, Sherri, my assistant, shared some exciting news. "Alexis, I don't know if you realize it or not, but I just turned my garage into a dance studio. In the town of Franklin where I live, many friends and neighbors started begging me to teach ballroom dancing to their children. After thinking about it and talking to my husband, we decided to put in a hardwood floor and have organized classes. Do you realize I have over sixty students now? My son and a couple of our team members help me teach."

"I can't believe it, Sherri!"

She added, "It is amazing what dancing is doing for my own children. They go out in the studio, turn on the music, and dance with each other. They act like they like one another and are getting along. Dancing is helping our family get closer together."

As I drove home, I shook my head in disbelief. I never thought we would have two ballroom studios in our area and that dance would become so popular. The affect on the community was overwhelming.

Autumn's West Side High Dance Team

Chapter 27

Dance and Romance

To tell the truth, in the beginning I feared that my dance program might encourage young people to get physically involved prematurely. But my worries dissolved as I witnessed them set worthy goals. Dancing did foster romance, but appropriately, opening doors for the future when the time was right.

After one concert I saw Julia standing free for a minute, so I took the moment to question her about something I'd been curious about for years. "Hey Julia, do you mind if I ask you about your relationship with Keith. I know you have been together a lot the last couple of years. You seem to like each other."

She smiled, slightly embarrassed. "There was a time when we became very serious. Then we stepped back and said, 'Wait a minute. We are too young for this. We have things we want to do, like college.' We decided to cool it off and keep it a friendship. Later, after we have done some of the things we want, we will reconsider our relationship."

I couldn't believe their mature decision and was proud of their self-control. Maybe it was the example of older students doing it right.

Although my daughter Laura had dated a lot of different boys from her ballroom group, by her senior year she lost her desire to date anyone but Adam. At practices they sat very close together, and sometimes Adam slipped an arm around her. In the spring, Laura opened up to me about their relationship.

"Mom, you know how everyone in our school seems to know if you've been kissed or not? Well, all my friends started giving Adam and me a hard time. Remember when Adam asked me to the Valentine dance? Kids would come up to us and say, 'I bet you're going to kiss her on Valentine's Day,' or 'February 14th is the big day.'

"It got to be a big joke. Finally Adam said to me, 'This will be your first kiss, won't it? You want it to be special, don't you?'

"'Yes,' I told him.

"'Well, why don't we drive up to kissing rock some night?' Adam suggested. Kissing rock is in a remote area about a half-hour north of Preston where two huge rocks leaning against each other look like people kissing."

I told her I had heard of the place.

She continued, "We started to make fun of the situation. I would say, 'It looks like a full moon tonight. We have to have a full moon.'"

"Adam would say, 'Too many clouds; we can't go tonight.' We were looking for just the right time, so no one would be suspicious. One night a school activity ended earlier than we thought, so we decided to make the drive. And that is where I got my first kiss—at kissing rock."

I smiled thinking of my own first kiss. At the end of my first date, the boy leaned over to me in the car. Not knowing what he was up to, I turned my head and he kissed the back of my head. We were both embarrassed, but I was especially annoyed that he would try something with my father in the front seat as our chauffeur.

Laura enjoyed dancing with Adam throughout the school year. Because they were especially good at lifts, I asked them to let me video them demonstrating lifts to use for teaching.

After a two-hour session, they were exhausted, but the end product was a valuable tool.

When the spring concert came, I watched my darling daughter light up with happiness as she performed with the team. Our big finale number concluded the evening as fifty students hit all kinds of poses in a V shape. Adam was in the center lifting Laura in the spectacular one-arm lift. The audience went crazy. An hour of general dancing followed with Laura dancing up a storm, and most especially with Adam.

After graduation, somewhat impatiently, Laura waited two years while Adam served a mission in Australia for our church. She attended Brigham Young University and dated other boys as Adam had encouraged her to do. In her eyes, however, none of them measured up to her dancing man.

When he came home, Laura and Adam quickly realized the old zing was still there, so Christmas day they made a trip to kissing rock where Adam got on his knees and proposed. He opened his coat to show a Christmas present label on his chest with the words, "To Laura, from Santa." Laura said he was the best gift she ever received. They were married for eternity in the Logan temple that spring, and, of course, included dancing at their reception. We also showed the video of them demonstrating lifts together.

Adam and Laura dancing at their wedding

Laura and Adam continued their education at BYU and called to report they had taken a country dancing class together and won fourth place in the country two-step at a competition with hundreds of students. I was happy they continued their dancing romance. I never dreamed it would catch hold of my son, Russell.

Having a well-toned body was very important to Russ, especially since he coveted the chance to do a lift routine. A weight-lifting class each year and heavy work on his grandfather's farm in the summers paid off in muscles that rivaled Mike's, the he-man who did my first lift routine. Because of Russell's strength and talent, I put him in adagio numbers his last two years of school.

In the three-couple lift routine of his senior year, Russell lifted his petite partner, Caroline, with masculine grace. Uniquely the girls twirled and rolled up in long, flowing scarves that made them look like mythical nymphs. They even used the scarves to pull the men around.

In one particularly effective lift, Caroline sat with a knee bent on Russell's right shoulder and her other leg extended horizontally as Russell made a dramatic turn. In another stunning maneuver Russ spun Caroline while lying sideways across his shoulder at a right angle with her arms and legs scissored. He reversed the spin to bring her down in shadow position. I watched Russ, a man's man, with fiendish delight as he danced to one of the most beautiful and romantic songs ever written.

Russell, not being the kind of person to share feelings, would never admit in high school that he liked ballroom. If he did say anything, it was mostly negative. But when he graduated and attended BYU, Russ called to say, "Mom, I know for a long time I gave you a hard time and acted like I did not care about dancing, but I love it! I'm glad I am taking dance classes now. Thanks, Mom. Thanks for teaching me how to dance."

Russ postponed college to become a missionary for our church for two years, and he loved the new culture he was exposed to in Mexico City. One of his converts showed him a few salsa moves, motivating him to buy some Latin music. When he came home and went back to college, Russell taught himself more steps off of YouTube and got involved in the weekly salsa club on campus. Whenever he came home to visit, you could catch him dancing around the house like a south-of-the-border native.

The following summer Russ dated Caroline, his former lift partner. During one warm evening

Russell taught her the salsa on her patio in the moonlight. Another date involved practicing all their old lifts, including the T-press, ending with more salsa on my deck roof. Although he and Caroline eventually parted, Russell learned that dancing was one of the best ways to please a woman. This is why his younger brother gave him the nickname of "Romance."

Many wonderful couples married after beginning their courtship in ballroom dance class. Some only dated a few times in high school, but dancing gave them something in common that brought them back together when the time was right.

A wedding announcement from Josh and Melissa gave me extreme happiness. My sober Josh, who loved the paso doble, married his paso partner. They attended my concert each year and boogied to frolicking tunes afterward. One spring, however, they created an unforgettable picture—three of them together, Josh, Melissa, and their sweet little baby girl held between them as they danced. It was priceless.

Josh confided to me, "Dancing is something we can share the rest of our lives. Melissa and I are closer because of it."

Josh and Melissa King dancing with
their baby after the concert

Caroline's older brother, Nate, had been
on the Latin team. Sometimes he danced with
Bracken. Years later I noticed Nate and Bracken
walking through town holding hands. I was
happy to see them together. Shortly thereafter I
received a wedding announcement from them.
They went on to have a large family.

Rusty was one of my three wrestlers who
did the T-press in a lift routine. He initially
decided to try out for ballroom in hopes that he
might be able to see more of a classy girl on the
Latin team named Rachael. Watching graceful
Rachael move around the room only made him

admire her more. He was very happy when she asked if she could hitch a ride each morning for class. In his senior year, although they were not partners, Rusty and Rachael had the chance to be in the same lift number. I saw them talking together often. Rusty asked her to the prom. Rachael continued her education and majored in dance at BYU, while Rusty went on a mission. When he came back, they started dating again, resulting in marriage.

A wedding announcement of special significance came from Claye, my popular Latin dancer who had moved to the Standard team and had fallen in love with Samantha. Samantha's family only lived a few houses down from me, so I was able to see Sam and Claye often when they came to visit during college breaks. We rejoiced when children were added to the union.

Samantha & Claye Stokes

Many of my students knew the following to be true:

Learning to dance is the way, if you please,
To get a young man right down on his knees.
How can he resist
A graceful young miss
Who moves 'cross the floor with such ease?

Later when computers made it possible for me to connect with former students through social networking, I asked them to tell me of their dancing history once they left high school. I received many emails from ballroom friends describing the affect of dancing in their lives. One boy wrote:

I do love to dance. I took several dance classes at BYU-Idaho and was on the team there for a year. I was recently asked to teach ballroom at my church daddy-daughter night. My wife has picked up a lot, and we dance every chance we get. We have been on several cruises where people just stop to watch us. We have even won prizes. It has been a great talent to have, and I am very thankful you helped me develop it. Thank you for imparting your time and talents, and my wife thanks you too. There is something magical about randomly dancing in our kitchen.

Jack

Brett, from my first team, sent the following email:

Alexis,
After high school, my mission, and my first year of college, I decided that I missed

dance. So I tried out for the Utah State University Ballroom Dance Team and made it. I danced with them for two years, competing in Las Vegas and Canada on the Standard team. I wasn't the best but the enjoyment I received from dancing was forever life changing, and I loved every minute of it. It will forever have a very positive effect on my life. When I was dating in college, it was so fun to know some basics in dance and actually be able to dance with a girl. It really impressed those I dated. I loved, and still do love, to dance.

While dancing in college, a neighbor girl asked me to be in a cabaret number with her for the church talent show. The judges loved it so much, they picked us to represent them in the regional talent show.

My wife really appreciates that I know how to dance. Every time we go to weddings or any type of dance, she loves to dance with me. As I hold her in my arms, I know that dancing is something special in our lives. I can tell from that sparkle in her eyes when she looks at me.

Thank you, Alexis, for the special thing you have given me.

Brett

Tiara and Brett Reeder

My goal in teaching dancing was to give teenagers a great time. But dancing had given them what most of us dream about—romance.

Chapter 28

Annual Concert

Running into a former student one day, he informed me about the latest going on in his life. Then he surprised me by saying, "It's funny how your perspective changes, Alexis. When I was on the team, you had us learn a big ending number for the concert each year. I used to think that the finale was kind of silly. But I was at your concert last spring as a member of the audience instead of as a participant, and I thought the finale was cool with all those formations. I don't know why I didn't like it before."

I laughed and said, "I'm glad you decided it was alright."

I loved teaching the finale! It was a challenge to be heard over fifty teenagers, but their excitement was energizing. Sometimes to get their attention, I would yell, "Are you ready?" A loud "Yeah" would follow before I put the music on for a run through. If they didn't holler back so I could hear, I would ask again until a more boisterous "Yeah" would echo.

We tried a different style each year—swing, foxtrot, Lindy hop, samba, New York hustle, etc. With such a large group we could do fancy formations. We had vertical lines pass through each other, horizontal lines where the students in the back ducked under the linked arms of the line moving back. Double circles turned different directions passing in and out to create stars. There were Xs that rotated, breaking into double Xs and passing through each other, as well as multiple diagonal lines that moved opposite ways.

If you could imagine it, we did it, including dramatic ripples, lifts and dips, random pop ups and arm swings, as well as many traditional steps.

I pictured things in my mind at home, but when I saw them in reality, it was even better. Sometimes the students came up with great ideas. If someone had a special talent, I tried to use them.

An especially popular finale was highlighted with Brandon doing a solo hip hop routine in the center with everyone sitting around on the floor making a kaleidoscope with their bodies. The finale was a dramatic pinnacle each year, resulting in a standing ovation.

At times I dedicated the ending number to special people. A tribute to Fred Astaire using a medley of songs from his movies ended one of our concerts. I had read a biography about him (*Puttin' on the Ritz*, by Peter J. Levinson) and was very impressed with Fred's drive and hard work that made him one of the greatest dancers of our age.

Another year I used a song about New York and dedicated it to my Uncle Alex whom I was named after. He was a good war buddy of my father's and was my New Yorker pen pal for thirty years before he died. He had spent his life helping disabled veterans.

When my first ballroom student passed away, I arranged a finale to pay homage to Lance Jensen. Lance accidentally drowned while swimming in a river in his early twenties. It was even more tragic because he was engaged to be married. At the concert I quoted a limerick I wrote about him years earlier.

There once was a shy boy named Lance
Who decided to learn how to dance.
But now he's not meek.
He's who all the girls seek.
And his life is full of romance.

I told the audience, "I have known for a long time that my ballroom students are some of the nicest kids in town and Lance was no exception. So, for our finale tonight we present in honor of him a dance called, "The Nicest Kids in Town." It was a lively swing the kids performed with enthusiasm.

Once in awhile we had a few surprises during the show, such as, during a swing when Alice squatted and her partner pulled her through his legs. As he did so, her skirt (that had an elastic waistband) caught in her heel and pulled down below her fanny when she stood. She immediately yanked the front fabric up, but didn't realize the back of her red skirt was still below her backside. She continued the dance unaware that her white bottom showed until the end of the dance.

There was the time Ada landed on her caboose with a thud when her fill-in partner didn't catch her in a fallback. Stunned and in pain, she missed a few more steps, then, hit a tenuous ending pose.

In a lift routine, Katie's shoe dropped off and she had to dance around on one tip toe.

Another crazy situation appeared as a girl went into a somersault. Her partner thought she was too slow, so he gave her a shove on the behind to make the pose on time.

Sometimes we invited fabulous, visiting soloists to participate. At one concert we had the BYU-Idaho country swing winners perform. They were very professional with high-speed steps and a multitude of lifts that the amateur would never even try. The crowds joined in clapping to the rhythm of the music while cheering at the top of their voices.

Occasionally a former student who went on to college would come back to dance a specialty. Skyler was asked to perform a rumba by one of my senior girls. Skyler was one of those rare individuals who not only had natural talent, but threw his heart and soul into getting as much ballroom in his life as he possibly could — a danceoholic. In high school he made up his own dances and taught classes for Autumn. After Skyler performed his rumba, I asked him to tell the audience what was going on at BYU-Idaho. He told about six students from Preston, including himself, who were dancing on the team up there.

Two of them were also assisting with high school teams.

Audiences not only enjoyed our spring concert, but they loved to kick up their heels for an hour afterwards during general dancing. It was good to see parents dancing with teenagers, past students with old friends, and older couples moving around the floor. My own children were as involved as the others.

Visiting with people before and after the show was an added bonus. One evening when Mr. Saunders, the choir director, came up to me, I said, "I sure enjoyed having your daughter on the team this year. I must admit though the highlight was watching you dance with her tonight."

He laughed, and said, "Oh really? It was a great show."

Mr. Saunders proved himself right. Singers do dance.

My tenth annual concert was particularly special. As I handed out programs at the door, many old students appeared with love in their eyes. I hugged each one, and memories swarmed around us. The concert went forward with my current students performing over fourteen numbers. After the finale made its traditional climax, I called each senior up to present him or her with a trophy topped with a dancing couple and acknowledged those who helped that year.

Suddenly Sarah, one of my first-year girls, took the microphone and began to speak. "In celebration of Alexis' ten-year anniversary of teaching ballroom dance here at Preston High School, we'd like those who have been her students to stand." At least a hundred people rose. Sarah went on, "We would like her first team members to come down." Eleven young people descended the bleachers.

Sarah handed the microphone to K'Lyn who approached with a small tree in a planter. K'Lyn spoke, "We can't do enough to express our appreciation to Alexis for the years she taught us to dance and live life to the fullest, but we would like to present her with this tree. It is symbolic of the seed she has planted in our community which will continue to grow and grow, blessing the lives of those around her.

My arms enveloped K'Lyn as I thanked her. Among the first-years present was Michelle, my first soloist; Brett who danced "The Blue Danube" with K'Lyn; Annie who had trouble keeping her skirt on, the bride in my first medley; Jeremiah King, the first of a long line of Kings; Nic who had edited my music for years; Cindy who performed in foreign countries with the

BYUI college team; Doug, a first class guy who talked Brett into trying out with him; Sarah, who broke her leg her senior year but healed in time to do our concert; and Autumn who had started her own studio. It was obvious that Autumn was well along in pregnancy. I asked her when she was due and she informed me in one week.

"Oh, Autumn, it must have been miserable for you to sit on those hard bleachers when you are about to have a baby any minute. That is a real sacrifice."

"I was fine, Alexis. I wouldn't miss this special night for anything. I wanted you to know how much I love you. Dancing has meant everything to me."

I squeezed her again. Touched by everyone's thoughtfulness, I stood there for a while speaking to friends. My brother, Matt, attending for the first time, hugged me and said, "I was late because I couldn't find a parking place. You didn't tell me the whole town would show up." He congratulated me and then danced around with his wife and three daughters.

I finally made my way over to Laura who was with her ballroom buddies including the boys who did a special birthday dance for me years before. It was a tradition for her group to meet each year at the concert, and I loved reuniting with them. The beautiful evening was topped off with enthusiasts flying around the gym to glorious rhythms, David and I included.

That night, after everyone left and I went home, I lay in bed a long time pondering. It amazed me how a little dancing could bring so much joy to so many people. My efforts to serve had probably done more for myself than any other person. I was like the tree and had grown tremendously over the years, and each leaf represented a friend I had made. I truly felt fulfilled. The annual concert provided a chance to see, once again, those who had become so dear to me.

Brandon's hip hop solo in the finale

Chapter 29

Ballroom Brad

We called our fifth child, fourth son, Brad. David's middle name was Bradley. So, this boy was named for him. Sometimes David teased me that he named Laura after a girl he dated in high school, rather than for the song that we listened to while we dated. That's when I would remind him that my old flame in college was named Brad.

My son Brad first started dancing with Autumn's group, the Smooth Swayers, when he was eleven years old along with my youngest daughter, Karrie. They both did well and seemed to like it.

Much to my chagrin, Brad refused to ballroom dance his first year of high school. At the start of his sophomore year I was heartbroken when Brad stubbornly announced, "I'm not going to try out for your team at all, so just get used to the idea, Mom!"

Previously, I went along peacefully when he said he wanted a year to adapt to high school before trying out. I wanted him to join for the right reasons, not because I wanted him to. But it made me sad to think of him missing out on this great chance to enjoy life to the hilt. I went to tryouts disheartened.

That same afternoon when Brad came home from school, he said many girls told him they were disappointed that he was not dancing. Brad was a good-looking, well-built blond who had a way with the girls. I hoped they could persuade him.

A week into tryouts, Brad handed me a CD player and demanded, "Mom, bring your dance music and get downstairs right now. You are teaching me the tryout numbers."

Casually I walked down the stairs, not letting on that I was doing cartwheels around the room in my mind. Trying to keep a straight face, I taught him each step. He caught on fast. Brad had his dad's natural smoothness and great rhythm. All right, maybe he inherited a little of it from me.

The next morning when he showed up for tryouts, several girls excitedly screamed his name, as though he were Robert Pattinson. He laughed, turned around, and walked out again. The girls ran after him dragging him back in. He loved the attention. Brad caught up like a pro and ended up on the Standard team. No one could deny that he was qualified.

Brad seemed to enjoy our class time. However, he was still fearful that his jock friends would persecute him when they saw him dance at the school basketball games.

At his first performance in the PHS gym, the amplified words came, "Ladies and Gentlemen, for your halftime entertainment, the Preston High Ballroom Dance Team." I watched excitedly when Brad made an entrance with the Standard team. The men were in tuxedo shirts and pants, silver vests and ties, and the girls in long, blue ballroom gowns with draping sleeves. A lovely slow waltz began, moving the couples with elegant grace in formations. The beautifully orchestrated tune from a popular movie, drew in the audience, then, turned into a Viennese waltz.

In rehearsals Brad's friend always gave him a high five when they passed each other during the dance. But in this performance his friend shook his head and chickened out. They both laughed. I noticed Brad was smiling a lot throughout.

In an abrupt peak in the music, the girls hit a pose with outstretched arms and each boy kneeling behind holding his partner's waist. As the music faded, the men dragged the women off the floor.

When we got home that night, Brad confessed, "Mom, I thought I was going to hate performing because I was so worried about what my friends thought. But they laughed with me and acted like I was cool. I made faces back at them during the whole thing. It was really fun, Mom. Performing is awesome!"

I was pleased he had made the discovery. I now had one more son living it up.

When Brad competed with the Standard team at the Gem State Dance Championship that year and saw the other impressive high school teams with perfect toplines and graceful rise and fall, he became even more pumped about ballroom. At home he confessed, "Mom, I truly love Standard dancing. I want to be a great dancer!"

I could not believe this was the same boy who refused to tryout last fall.

One of my favorite medleys I taught while Brad was in my program had music from a movie, which spoofed a Prince and Princess marrying happily ever after. We dressed the girls in beautiful, white and royal blue ballroom gowns and placed tiaras in their hair. The men were in gold Prince Charming doublets. At one point during the music, each man pulled a flower from under his coat, knelt, and presented it to the lady. The girls danced around with the flowers, then threw them in the air at a high point in the music. Even though it was corny, Brad liked pretending to be a prince.

Over time Brad's good looks and height increased, reaching six-foot-two, and he became one the most graceful Standard men in our team history. Alongside him, Priscilla began to stand out. She was as pretty as he was handsome. Priscilla's parents had also met on the BYU dance team in college. Both blessed with deliciously-long legs, Brad and Priscilla had natural rhythm and coordination that was in their blood. When Priscilla first came in as a freshman, Brad acted like he was not interested in dancing with her. But something happened to change his mind.

At home he confided, "Mom, you know how Priscilla jumped in and danced with me when my partner wasn't there this morning?"

"Yes."

"Well, I couldn't believe how fast she picked up the dance and followed perfectly in a spot she had never done before. She's incredible!"

I was glad to see him recognize her talents as I had. He now started to ask her to be his partner in other routines.

Initially, I told Brad and Liz that they could do a quickstep solo their senior year. He and Liz were good friends having grown up together in the same neighborhood. She was a very pretty, talented blond. But seeing Priscilla blossom, I tried to think of a way to include both girls.

Then I came up with the idea to have a quickstep duet. I could put Brad and Priscilla together, as they were more the right height, and ask another boy to work with Liz. During the routine I could have the men switch partners several times. Hopefully, that would keep everyone happy and add a lot of interest to the dance.

The partner I wanted for Liz was a gifted young man on the Latin team. At the beginning of the year I called him up and said, "Hey, Dixon, Would you like to be in a Standard specialty number?"

Suspicious, he said, "Are you planning to put me on the Standard team this year? If you are, I am going to quit. I will only make time for ballroom if you keep me on the Latin team."

"Oh, Dixon, I still plan on having you with Latin. I just thought you might like the challenge of trying something new. I think you will pick up the quickstep really well."

"Oh, good." He sighed, relieved to keep his Latin position. "Sure, I'll give it a try. But remember, I still want to be on the Latin team."

I laughed. "Don't worry. And I promise that you are going to love this number. You will be dancing with Liz."

He seemed happy about his partner. But I got vibes that he was underestimating the treat he was in for with the quickstep.

The vision opened up at our first rehearsal where I began with some elegant International steps that took them around the room in a hurry. They felt the exhilarating flow of the high-speed travel. Then at opposite corners I had the couples do a promenade run passing each other. It went step hop, quick & quick, kick 2,3,4, switch, switch, step, leap.

The kids laughed when they messed up, attempting the jump over and over until they could do it in unison. I ran right along with them counting. At the open gym door, a custodian paused to watch and yelled, "Hey, can I get lessons like that? I want to learn to dance too!"

Walking out of breath to rest on the side, I looked at Dixon's smiling face and said, "Well, you better watch out, Dixon, we just might convert you to Standard dancing."

He smiled and said, "I think you have."

I looked forward to the duet practices so I could reveal the next brainwave that came to me. After the leaping pass, they circled around moving to the center. The girls spun to do silly poses with a different man. Trading back, the couples did polka turns around each other, then a spinning lift. Promenade skips took them in opposite vertical directions. Twirling alternating hops were next. In the center the girls traded again and the men stepped back for a leap over the women's heads.

They rippled the girls up into a lift. Brad set Liz down, but Dixon kept turning Priscilla. Liz pointed her finger on a pulsing sound, gesturing for Dixon to put Priscilla down. So he threw Priscilla at Brad who caught her like a bouquet of flowers. Brad backed away with the momentum while Liz pushed Dixon backward like an angry hussy. The teasing interactions were laughable. With a running weave toward each other, the couples traded partners with a hop, skip slide maneuver.

The end of the dance came with the girls running up the backs of their men being lifted under arms above the boys for a spin. They came down, twirled, and hit a pose with arms out to the last line, "I'm a dancin' fool. Yeah!"

Seeing Brad with a face like he was in seventh heaven was my reward. It was like having a piece of my favorite strawberry, cream cheese pie each time they danced. When my husband saw it performed, he leaned over to say, "I think that's my favorite of all the dances you've ever done."

"It's mine, too."

Brad, a "dancin' fool," was bitten by the bug—a bug that had already latched onto my youngest child, Karrie.

Standard Medley, Brad (center), Liz
on his right, Priscilla above him

Brad Beckstead, Priscilla Hobbs,
Liz Child, Dixon Bowles – dancin' fools

Chapter 30

Carrying on the Tradition

At home as a little girl, my daughter Karrie often put on music, danced around the living room, and asked for my critique. "You did very well." I would respond. "I think you are a great dancer."

Then she would reply, "Oh, Mom, you are just saying that because you're my mother. You wouldn't say anything different."

I would try to tell her that even if I weren't her mother I would say the same thing. But she wouldn't believe me.

When Karrie was in eighth grade, she competed with Sherri's son at a competition in the junior category. To our surprise they received first place in the cha-cha among a large group of kids their age. They were overjoyed, and I was too. "See, Karrie," I announced. "I told you that you were a great dancer. Now do you believe me?"

She gave me a look of "well maybe."

As fate would have it, my youngest, who had been lifted by her older brothers as a practice subject, who came to classes with me because she wanted to watch, who begged me to dance with her around the living room and at the concert as a little girl, and who wanted to be on my team more than anything in the world, had the misfortune to have scoliosis. Her spine began to form the shape of an 'S.' Back surgery in her freshman year required that she refrain from any type of sport or dancing for six months. It was a terrible disappointment to her. The surgery was horribly painful, and she missed school for a month.

The good news was that the doctor was able to successfully fix her curved spine by putting rods and screws in it, making it possible for her to stand up straight again and get on with the love of her life—ballroom dancing.

As soon as the doctor gave her the okay to start physical activity once more, I signed her and Brad up for private lessons with a couple who had taken over the Utah State University team in Logan, Utah. Karrie and Brad improved their technique and worked on competition numbers becoming better friends in the process.

Karrie made the Standard team as a sophomore, happy to finally live her dream. We were all shocked when Karrie could be thrown in a backward 360-degree maneuver during the Lindy Hop routine with no back problems. Modern medicine was a marvel.

After her first performance in a beautiful, romantic medley clothed in a scintillating gown of blue velvet and flared organza, Karrie touched her long, white evening gloves and let her joy spill out, "Oh, Mom, you know I am mostly a casual-type person who likes to wear blue jeans, but there is nothing like dancing in a dress that makes you feel like a princess. I love being a princess! I decided tonight that I was going to dance with all the grace of a queen. Did I look like it?"

"Oh Karrie, you did. In fact, your dance brought tears to my eyes. You were exquisite."

"Thanks, Mom."

Meanwhile in her studio classes, Autumn noticed how good Karrie was with younger children who needed help. So, Autumn asked Karrie to teach two ballroom classes for her studio. Karrie had the most fun picking out music and creating dances while bouncing around my living room with her headphones on. Partway into the year she revealed the difficulties of the task to me.

"Mom, teaching eight to eleven year olds is not easy. Just getting them to connect with each other is a pain. The girls can be so mean and act like the boys have cooties. They say things out loud like, 'I'm not touching him!'"

"Then I find myself saying, 'This is ballroom, you have to touch.' For awhile they did the steps with their arms straight at their sides defiantly."

"One day when we finished up the swing number, I gave them each a different ending pose. I told this one girl to put her hands on a boy's shoulder and bend her knee with her foot up behind. The girl immediately yelled, 'I'm not doing it! It's princessy!'"

At this point I fell on the couch holding my stomach with laughter visualizing the situation. Here Karrie had told me she loved feeling like a princess, and this little girl wanted nothing to do with it.

Karrie continued, "I made her do it anyway. You know how hard I have worked to make up routines to teach, but they can't do anything. I have to simplify everything, because even the most basic moves baffle them."

"When I wanted to start teaching them a mambo, they were terribly stiff and mal-coordinated. Finally, I came up with the idea of getting the action out of them by convincing them it was like stepping on a bug. I explained, 'It is like this—squash that bug, squash that bug.' I stepped forward with my left foot, replaced my weight and stepped back with my right foot and replaced my weight again as I said the words. The children had so much fun yelling out 'squash that bug,' to the step that they continued to repeat it for the whole hour of class. I couldn't get them to quit. I thought I would lose my mind. I have to admit, though, my strategy did help them learn the basic mambo step."

I imagined a class full of children howling "squash that bug" for an hour and wondered how she was able to deal with it. She had remarkable patience.

Karrie and I attended a performance of her students at a church ball on the west side of the valley later that year. Entering the gym, the room was packed with dancing souls, a large portion in colorful floorshow costumes. Some were doing a line dance, others swayed in ballroom style, while many experimented in their own artistic way. There was excitement in the air.

When the floorshow began, Autumn's West Side High School Ballroom Team performed a clever swing and samba, well choreographed and executed. Then Karrie's groups entered with movements of beginners, but they had their steps down and were relishing the attention. After the show, all participants joined in with friends and parents.

Karrie leaned over to me and spoke in my ear, "Look what you started, Mom."

My heart overflowed as I observed everyone having a good time. I knew it wasn't me, but Karrie and Autumn carrying on the tradition.

In Karrie's junior year, I picked out a striking song and worked hard at putting together a tango for the Standard team. I could hardly wait to begin instruction. I first demonstrated the tango hold by grabbing a nearby boy. "Now remember that the girl holds her left arm and fingers out straight along the backside of the fellow's arm with the thumb under his arm. Be sure the thumb is not in his armpit. I showed the consequences.

The boy leaped away instantaneously. "Hey, I'm ticklish!" he hollered.

"Now there are two dances during which you do not smile—the tango and the paso doble. I want you, however, to put some drama and suave into your expression." I had them practice the basic step in a circle, remembering my dance class with David in college. When I felt they were getting the hang of the tango movement, I began the routine.

After a rippling press-line beginning, I had each girl put her hand on the man's chest and push him backward in staccato fashion. Checks and pivots followed, with the men rippling the women upside down in a diagonal. As they ran through it with music, I yelled out, "Don't smile!"

Bursts of laughter.

At home I asked Karrie how she liked the tango. "Oh, Mom, it is great. I tried hard to keep a straight face, but I couldn't with my shy partner trying to give me a sensual, Zorro look. It was hilarious!"

We worked hard to polish the number and took it to the Gem State Dance Competition in February, where they won third place in their category. The United States Dance Association was the host, turning it into a National event for Youth Showtime numbers, which made it more prestigious.

A month or so later, Karrie came home from school anxious to share some news with me. "Mom, I had to give a persuasive presentation in my Speech class, so I tried to persuade the class to learn ballroom dancing."

"Karrie, I wish I had heard it. Would you repeat it for me?"

"Sure, Mom. Here it comes."

I braced myself, expecting a treat. Karrie had the brains of her father, a playful personality, and a passion for dancing that was sure to make it a winner.

"With TV shows on the air like "Dancing with the Stars" and "So You Think You Can Dance," ballroom dancing is becoming increasingly popular. It is actually being considered for an Olympic sport. Now, why am I telling you this? I want you to know how amazing ballroom dancing is and hope you will try it.

"I have been doing ballroom dancing for eight years, and I can honestly say that it is fantastic! If all of you give it a chance, you will love it!

"There are three reasons why ballroom is amazing. First, it is easy to learn. Second, you get to meet hot guys or hot girls. Third, you and your partner are one.

"First, it is easy to learn. You can do slow or fast dances. You can do easy or hard steps. There are Bronze steps for beginners and Gold steps for the more advanced dancer. It is nice—easy for beginners or more challenging if you wish to go farther.

"Second, you get to meet hot guys and hot girls. What can be better than hanging out with hot guys or girls? You get to go to class, meet people, and be with friends.

"Third, you and your partner are one. The thing that makes ballroom dancing unique is that two people dance as one. In other forms of dancing you may pretend to be a tree or a flower. There is nothing more beautiful than two people moving in complete unison.

"So to conclude, ballroom dancing is easy, you make good friends, and it is flat out amazing to glide around the floor with someone else. I promise every single one of you that if you give ballroom dance a chance, you will love it. There is a reason why it is becoming extremely popular."

"Mom, when it was all over, my teacher who has studied jazz and modern dancing said to me, 'I've been pretending to be a tree or flower for ten years.' It was funny."

I thanked Karrie for promoting my true love. I couldn't have said it better myself.

She danced a graceful lift routine in her senior year that brought tears to my eyes. We were all amazed when she used her persuasive power to talk her father into doing a fancy quickstep solo. Practices proved that the old boy still had it in him. In the music they chose, a girl sang, "Gimme some rhythm, daddy," then a man sang, "Gimme some rhythm, baby." It was cute to see them bouncing around together to the lively tune. The time spent together in practice was choice, a sweet memory to keep forever.

When people asked Karrie what she wanted to do after high school, she replied, "I'm going to BYU in Provo and try to make the ballroom dance team. I want to carry on the tradition."

Karrie Beckstead with Marco Crosland
in a Charleston ending pose

Chapter 31

Dancing Families

After years of hoping and praying for the right girl to come along for my son Dave, who was twenty-seven years old and in his third year of medical school at Ohio State, I was very happy when he called to say he was getting serious about a nursing student named Megan. He described several dates where he taught Megan the swing, cha-cha, and the foxtrot. Discovering how fun dancing could be, she promptly went out and bought some dance shoes.

Eventually, Dave proposed marriage and our family flew out to Columbus for the ceremony. I wept when Dave and Megan stared into each other's eyes with a look of love one reads about in fairy tales. My mother and father had looked at each other that way all the years I was growing up.

The reception started off with a special bride-and-groom foxtrot. Then I had the fun of waltzing with my son, while Megan danced with her father. Dave was easy to follow and we basically showed off. Looking over my shoulder, I saw Brad and Karrie waltzing. My son, Russell, didn't want to be left out and found a partner as well. Later, I enjoyed a turn with my husband, and he also danced with Karrie. It was appropriate that this took place at a Beckstead wedding, for dancing was part of our lives. It increased the joy of the occasion.

In the little town of Preston, Idaho, dancing became a tradition for many families and brought them closer together. Almost every year two siblings were on the team at once, and it was not uncommon for three, four, or five brothers and sisters in a family to come through the program. But I was surprised when a senior boy approached me and asked if he could do the lift routine with his younger sister. "You want your sister to be your partner?" I asked in disbelief.

His sister came up in time to say, "Yes, we think it will be fun. We can get in extra practice time at home."

"It's fine with me," I responded. This was something that had never happened before in my class, but I thought it was great. They were both excellent for the part. He was big shouldered and strong; she was petite and graceful.

I loved the moves in that three-couple number. Each girl ran to her man and leaped while the man caught her by one arm around the middle as she curled like a ball. Then he dragged her by one leg and lifted her to spin. When the spin was reversed, the girl bent backwards curling around the man, ending to rest on his knees—very pretty. The audience at the Jr. High assembly particularly seemed to like the number.

After that, many brothers and sisters chose to dance together. One brother requested his sister as a partner for a country swing specialty. Another brother and sister danced a waltz, while others paired for the finale. I was shocked when my son, Brad, wanted to perform a medley with his sister, Karrie.

One year, in particular, set a record for sibling dancing. We had three brother/sister sets, as well as three Crosland brothers and three Larson brothers on the A teams at the same time. They enjoyed the camaraderie of driving to practices together and working on the same numbers.

One day when I ran into Richard King, he asked, "Alexis, do you realize you've had a King on your team every year since you started? That's fourteen years."

"That's right." It finally dawned on me. "Your family is a ballroom tradition."

"My brother, Jeremiah, was on your first team, then my sister, Tosha. She did a paso doble solo with Claye—remember?"

"I do. In one finale we had Tosha stand above two rows of men who flipped her full length over and over along the line to pose on a boy's shoulders. I was nervous because it never once worked right in practice and I held my breath at the concert. But it came off perfectly."

"I remember that," said Rich. "Then there was my brother, Josh. He ended up marrying his dance partner, Melissa."

"Jason was next. He did a great foxtrot solo with Erica to 'Kick in the Head,'" I remembered.

Mentally I reviewed the dance where Erica pretended to kick Jason in the head. He reeled and fell down on the ground. The dance ended with her putting her foot on his back and posing with her hand on her hair. The audience always laughed at the end. Erica and Jason were part of Laura's close-knit dating group.

Continuing about Jason, I said, "That lift routine he did with Stephanie to help her with her senior project was gorgeous."

"Yeah, it was awesome. I came next," he said exultantly. "You had me do a solo Viennese waltz with Serina when I was a junior. I don't know if you were aware of it or not, but Serina and my older brother had been girlfriend and boyfriend for a long time. When Serina dumped my brother, I thought she treated him terribly, making me really angry. Then you asked me to solo with her. I wanted to solo more than anything, but I didn't know if I could stand dancing with someone I was upset with. Serina seemed uncomfortable about it too. But it all worked out. After dancing with her so much, I couldn't be mad at her anymore. I was able to forgive her, and we ended up becoming really good friends."

"Oh Rich, I had no idea any of this was going on or that either of you felt that way," I exclaimed. "Your Viennese waltz solo was beautiful with a lovely music box feel. I thought it was good for both of you."

He nodded in agreement. "I was glad you asked me to do that lift number my senior year. Now my younger sister, Taylee, is a senior and she is doing a cha-cha duet."

"How many more Kings are there?" I inquired.

"I have one more sister after Taylee, making seven.

I wanted to clarify something and said, "You know, Richard, some people might think that I play favorites with families, but over the years I have noticed that coordination runs in families. I put the Kings on the team because you each had good rhythm and talent. You have a wonderful family, Rich."

Rich may not have realized it, but his family name was a perfect symbol. Ballroom dancing makes you feel like a king.

Running into the father of another dancing family at a parent teacher conference, I had to kid him. "Did you know we are going to call you the Dancing Croslands? With Rico in my group, that makes eight of your children that have been on the ballroom team now."

Mr. Crosland smiled, "Yeah, that is something, isn't it? My wife and I think it is great!"

Mrs. Crosland had been to Italy and fell in love with the place. When she married, she talked her husband into giving their eleven children Italian names. A very unusual family, they lived up in the canyon, taught their children to work hard, and enjoyed the outdoor life. Mr. Crosland kept his children occupied by building a multi-room tree house like *Swiss Family Robinson*.

I wanted to review. "Let's see. First, there was beautiful Malia. She did a foxtrot solo as a junior to a song called 'Dancing in The Dark,' which I chose because my husband and I practiced in the dark in college. Malia also danced a tango solo as a senior.

Mr. Crosland remarked, "You remember she married her dance partner from the BYU-Idaho team, don't you?"

"Of course. I was tickled about that."

"Then there was Giovanni," he continued. "Gio married Kristina, Sherri's daughter. They did several numbers together in high school."

I added, "A few years after they graduated, Gio and some friends put together a specialty number, and we let them perform it at the concert. He is a great guy. I hear he's majoring in pre-med?"

"That's right," said Mr. Crosland. "Arianna came after him."

"She helped teach the B team and did a lift routine as a senior," I recalled. "You've broken the record, though. You are the only family to have four children on the dance team all at once.

Armando was on the Standard team at the same time Teresina was on the Latin team and your twins, Marco and Mario, were in the backup group."

"Yeah, I bet that doesn't happen very often," he commented.

I continued. "I loved Armando's two solos—the waltz he did with Paige, and the tango he danced with Ariel. That tango was unique—the way we had Ariel snap a big Spanish fan open and closed throughout the number."

I kept going, "Marco did a beautiful waltz solo with Priscilla, and Mario was in a lift routine when they were seniors. Because your kids were so good, I had them filling in for missing people all the time. They danced more than all the other students."

"Yeah, you sure had them busy. I'm certain my two youngest children will want to try out in a few years, too," added Mr. Crosland.

The Crosland kids were very special to me. I loved them like my own children and deemed it an honor to work with them.

Dancing also brought children closer to their parents. Liz came to me about March of her senior year and said, "Alexis, you know the Junior Miss Pageant is in a couple of months. Since I am the

Junior Miss, I am supposed to come up with some kind of entertainment for the audience while the judges are making their decision. I thought it would be nice if you would teach my father and me a waltz to perform. My dad agreed to do it if you will help us. I found an amazing song I'd like to use."

"Liz, I would love to. Let me see what I can put together. Our specialties are finished, so the gym is free before rehearsals. Is your father willing to come in at 6:30 in the morning?"

"Yes, he is."

"You have a nice dad, Liz. He sure is brave."

I was happy to do something for them. Liz lived around the corner from me, and her mother Karen was my best friend. I had taught three of Karen's other children, as well.

At home I played the song and fell in love with the romantic tune instantly, feeling inspiration from it. I waltzed around my family room and quickly arranged the steps, realizing that this would be something beautiful.

At our first practice, Robert joked that his daughter's gracefulness came from her mother, not from him. Although willing, Robert was a little unsure of himself. Liz, however, fluttered like a dove around him enchantingly. With continued rehearsals and memorization of the steps, Robert began to loosen up and even agreed to try a few simple lifts. Being very robust, he spun his daughter effortlessly to the apropos words describing a lovely woman who danced.

When I ran into Liz's mother one afternoon, she informed me, "Robert loves dancing! He says he feels like Fred Astaire. Thank you for sacrificing your time for them."

"Oh, don't worry about that. I am enjoying working with them."

Greatly satisfied with the final product, I asked if they would be willing to do a preview performance at our year-end concert. Glad to have another opportunity to exhibit, they accepted the invitation. Because many people knew the family from their active involvement in the community, I felt it would be well received.

At our closing show, it was the sweetest thing to see the father and daughter walk out on the floor together, Robert in a classy tux and Liz dressed in a beautiful purple ballroom gown trimmed with feathers. Liz had the most attractive smile God could bless a person with and the joy of being with her Dad emanated from her. Robert looked stately and elegant as the dance began. It was exciting to see the change in Robert from the first practice, he now looked polished. It was an excellent showpiece for Liz who floated around her dad like an angel. The audience let out a soft "ah," touched by the scene that ended with Liz in a dip. It even brought tears to some eyes.

Liz was graduating in a few short weeks and would going off to college in the summer. How could Robert stand to see his daughter leave home? How could I stand not to have her in my program any longer? One thing was certain, we would always hold dear the memory of the magical dance she and her father shared together.

The magic repeated itself the following year when Priscilla became the next Junior Miss. She had won by doing an incredible solo Latin medley. Wanting to continue Liz's tradition, Priscilla arranged a number with her father. Priscilla's father, with past experience dancing at BYU, and Priscilla, with a godly gift, performed a divine waltz at my concert that plucked every heartstring. What a wonderful way for father and daughter to say they were important to each other. As she, too, would be leaving soon, it was a special way to say goodbye.

Priscilla and her father, Randy Hobbs
dancing their waltz solo

Malia Crosland, the first of a long line of
Croslands, and Shawn Beardall, one of five
dancing Beardalls. Mac, in the background,
had three siblings on the team.

Chapter 32

Spiritual Expression

When Leanne moved up from the B team to the Latin team, she visited with me at the beginning of the year, "Alexis, we had so much fun at the pizza measuring party. Thanks for inviting everyone over to your house. I love ballroom dancing so much. The whole day is better when I come to practice. I was just talking to some of the girls. You know how we always pray before performances? Well, we wondered if we could pray before class starts. Don't you think that would be a nice way to start out the day?"

"Leanne, I love that idea. I haven't done that before because I worried it might bother someone. But if everyone agrees to it, I don't see why we shouldn't. When I was in college we used to have a thought and prayer before class. Maybe we should have a message too."

Leanne liked the suggestion. I approached the students with the idea, and they all voted in favor. It became an uplifting part of our class.

Our messages were of an ethical nature. I tried not to make them religious. But one day I asked myself, why should I be inhibited about giving credit where it's due? Everyone in my group belongs to my church. I'm going to share the feelings of my heart."

So one morning I surprised everyone by saying, "For our message today, I will tell you how I choreograph a dance." Suddenly they were all ears.

"At first my mind is blank, so I get on my knees and pray to my Father in Heaven to help me make up a dance that you will like. Then, I go to work. Listening to the music, ideas begin popping into my head, pictures come in my mind, and formations appear. I suddenly know what to do. It isn't me. I'm not capable. I know where it comes from.

"Just as God is able to help me make up a dance, I know that he can help you perform it to the best of your ability if you ask him.

"Some people might think, 'Why would God care about a dance?'

"God knows that the arts make our lives beautiful and exciting. They give us quality of life. He wants that for us. So I hope you will seek his aid in becoming better dancers."

Thereafter, the students prayed for the Lord to help them to do well. Making God part of our dance experience not only increased our ability, but our joy in sharing our talents.

Besides the Lord inspiring me in my choreography, an experience at one of our performances proved to me that God wants us to dance. When the boys' basketball team qualified for the district championship held in Pocatello, a bus was provided for us to drive up and dance for the halftime. As I parked at the school that night and climbed out of my car, I made the decision to leave my purse under the seat so I wouldn't have to haul it around with me at the game. But a very strong thought came to my mind, "Take your purse." I considered the annoyance of hauling it around, but the thought had been so strong that I decided to take my bag with me.

After the students loaded the bus and we made the hour-long drive to Pocatello, I was about to leave my purse on the bus, but again I got another strong thought, "Take your purse." I remember consciously saying, "Oh all right, I'll take my bag."

About five minutes before the halftime, I went out into the hall to make sure that my students were all costumed and ready to go when Maria ran up to me frantic. The front seam of her dress was split open from the bust down, giving us a full view of her underwear. "Alexis, look what happened! I was practicing a slide under my partner's legs, but he accidentally stepped on my dress and tore it." I walked over and held the seams shut, suddenly remembering that I had a box of safety pins in my purse.

"Don't worry, Maria. We will just pin it for now. You can still go on and no one will mind." I hastily put in a row of safety pins that held her dress together, and she went on like nothing happened. Well …she was blushing more than usual. Nobody said a thing about her metallic costume.

What if I had not brought my purse? I really didn't want to bring it that night. I felt the prompting was from a higher source—someone who wanted that sweet little girl to dance that night. It would have been heartbreaking if she couldn't perform. Remembering the strength of the impressions I received, I felt God wanted her to dance.

We had a special experience where dancing helped the audience feel closer to God. A month before Christmas I met three of my ballroom students after school. "Thank you for agreeing to be in this nativity scene for our church Christmas party," I told them. "The activities chairman gave me some beautiful music we will use. She wants this to be a dancing nativity."

"Kara, because of your ballet training, I want you to be the angel. We will start out with you dancing around on the stage. I'll let you choreograph your own routine because you are so experienced." Kara would be in a production of "The Nutcracker" at the community theatre that Christmas as well, and I knew she would do an incredible job.

I went on. "Skyler will be Joseph, and Jamie will be Mary." Skyler was one of my best dancers that year and was always willing to try anything. Jamie looked like a perfect Mary—a beautiful girl with long, wavy brown hair and glowing countenance.

I held out a bundle. "This wrapped up doll will be baby Jesus," I explained. "Now throughout this, I want both of you to look at this baby like it is the real Jesus. I want your love for the Savior to show in your eyes. Try to think what it might be like to actually be Joseph and Mary with the Christ Child.

You will both start at the back of the room and dance up the middle aisle. First, I want Mary to take the baby, spin forward and hold the baby up to the sky like he is a gift from heaven. Sway side to side looking at the child, then spin back to Joseph.

Now Joseph takes the baby and repeats the same steps as Mary. I Ie hands the baby to Mary and moves up the aisle with his wife. In the center of the aisle Joseph rolls Mary out, you both look at one another, and Mary rolls in for an under-arm lift." We practiced it up to that point several times.

"By now you are in front of the stage. Mary dances off to the right alone with the baby." I showed Jamie her steps. "Now I want Skyler to take Jesus and dance off to the left alone." As we practiced, I felt a precious feeling come over me. To see the sweet look on the faces of those young people as they moved around with that bundle pierced me to the soul.

"Now you both come together in one last lift before walking up the stairs to the stage. Mary hands the baby to Joseph, and he backs over to the side. At this point, I want the angel and Mary to dance together. Each of you put your right arm up and circle like a maypole. Spin around and circle the other way. Now leap across the stage changing sides like you are filled with 'tidings of great joy which shall be to all people.'" We went through it over and over.

I continued my instruction, "Mary, now returns to Joseph. Together you walk to the manger at the back of the stage while little children come in with the angel spinning about. Mary holds the baby up in the air as the little kids kneel, and then she places baby Jesus in the manger."

When the night of the performance came, I was convinced this would be a nativity few people would forget. With all the lights out except for a spotlight on the stage, Kara, my angel, entered in a flowing white gown, her soft, light-brown hair hanging down past her waist with golden garland encircling her head. She began to gracefully dance about the stage en pointe to "Away in a Manger." The orchestrated music was wispy like wind. The angel moved down the stairs toward Mary and Joseph, the spotlight following to highlight Jamie and Skyler standing there together, dressed in soft blue and off-white.

The angel backed away as they began their dance. The couple looked like you would imagine Joseph and Mary to appear—goodly and noble. I watched the audience, and witnessed the spirit of the event capture them. It was in their eyes as Mary and the angel danced together on stage, and as the innocent little children gathered near with the music ending like the sound of wind through a chime.

The dancing nativity made us all feel like we were part of that amazing night when the Son of God was born, filling us with all the emotion and glory of that moment in a deeper way than we had ever felt before.

Performing the nativity had showed how God loved us. To follow that, I wanted to express my love for God by making up a special dance to praise his name. I picked out a modern version of a song written by Beethoven that said what I felt.

As I gathered the Latin team around to teach the number, I told them, "The words to this song rejoice in the Lord. Here is your chance to dance before the Lord with all your might just like King David of old. I have choreographed the dance to fit the words, so it is important that you know them." The first verse of the adapted English lyrics went like this:

Joyful, Joyful, Lord we adore thee
God of Glory, Lord of Love
Hearts unfold like flowers before thee
Hail thee as the Son above.
Melt the clouds of sin and sadness
Drive the dark of doubt away
Giver of immortal gladness
Fill us with the light of day.

We did funk moves for the first fourth of the dance. Then the dancers moved to a half circle to do the hustle. After the men flipped their partners 360 degrees over their backs, they all moved into two lines, caught the girls in their arms, and threw them in the air as the girls did a log roll. When a line came in the next verse, "The Father of Love is rising o'er us," I had the boys pull the girls through their legs and lift them in the air by their waists. The women circled their arms. When they moved to one horizontal line, a dancer suggested that we have each girl do a somersault over the men's joined arms. I said, "I can't believe it. Do you know what the words are now? 'He watches over everything.' That would be perfect to put right there." The students grinned.

Crowds loved the number each time it was performed, but our highlight came the night of the Gem State Competition. As the Latin team ran down from the audience dressed in colorful, funky, teenage street clothes, I gave them my last words, "Tonight I want you to give it all you've got. Don't hold anything back."

I stood by the music tech and watched them enter with flip flops, worms, jumping, spinning, and shouting to a thumping beat. They danced with fire in their souls. "Joyful, Joyful, Lord we adore thee," rang out. They moved with their own special personalities and interpretations. At one point they moved to a horizontal line to do arm ripples, syncopated steps with their heads flipping, then, flea hops as one. The girls backed away to run and flip over the men's arms, then leaped to a new formation.

The audience cheered throughout. Inwardly I prayed, "I did it for you, Lord! This one's for you! Thank you for everything!" The spirit of love in the room was powerful. I felt God was pleased.

The dance ended with everyone leaping into lift poses then changing the position in a ripple on the last three beats to "Light of Day." Two girls arched, standing on their partners' knees. Simultaneously, the center man slid his partner through his legs. Then the girl spun in a circle, lying sideways with her head in her hand, as her partner did a handstand, flipped back to standing, and knelt with his arms held up in a

'V.' The dancers ran off the floor to deafening applause. Chills ran up and down my spine. Moved to tears, my team's performance had helped me express my adoration.

My joyful dancers

Chapter 33

The Ripple Effect

The example set in Preston became a lighthouse to other communities. As ballroom dance students went out into the world, they brought their reputation with them and shared their expertise in the places they settled. It was an inevitable ripple effect.

Several years after Sherri became my assistant, she had great news to tell me: "I have a sister named, Debbie, who lives in Fallon, Nevada. I told her about our dance group here, and it motivated her to start a high school team in Fallon, since she had college dance training. This is her first year, and she says it is going really well."

"Oh Sherri, I am so happy to hear it. Tell her I'd be happy to help her any way I can."

I recalled the performance I did in Fallon, Nevada many years ago on our college tour. I had never thought there would be a team there one day.

Sherri continued, "Debbie wants to bring her group up for the Gem State Dance Competition in February, and we thought it would be nice if the Fallon team could stop here in Preston on their way up to the competition. We could arrange a potluck supper for them together with our students, have a fun casual dance afterwards, and then let them stay overnight with Preston host families. They would drive up to compete the next day."

"Sherri, that will be a good way to motivate both groups. Let's do it. Tell Debbie it is fine with me."

When the Fallon team showed up, we had a grand time mingling and getting to know each other. After dinner the teenagers trotted with linked arms to Cotton-Eye Joe, gyrated to country line dances, and boogied to ballroom tunes and popular hip hop songs. Both schools tried to mix, so no one was left out. They didn't want the fun to stop.

We finally assigned the visitors to their adopted families who took them home overnight. The next morning at practice both groups displayed their competition numbers, trying hard to impress each other. Later that evening at the competition, we cheered for the Fallon team when they performed, and they cheered for us. It was nice to make new friends. We all enjoyed the exchange so much that we continued the tradition for many years.

Fallon High School started having ballroom dance classes as part of their P.E. curriculum. In talking to Debbie's students, I could see all the same side effects I had seen in my own students, including an increase of self-esteem, development of character, and the formation of solid friendships. Their whole town got involved with dance events, enlivening the Fallon community.

Joanna was part of the ripple effect. Years after she had graduated I received a phone call from her, and I asked her where she was living and what she was doing.

"Well, I am in Colorado," she replied. "I am married and have a cute little baby. One day my husband and I went out for dinner and dancing, and a man came up to us who had been watching us dance. He introduced himself as a high school principal in the area. After talking to us, he asked if we would like to start a ballroom dance team at his school. My husband and I decided to go ahead with it."

"Joanna that is fabulous! You will do a tremendous job," I responded.

"I need your help, Alexis. Tell me how you run your program. I would love to get your advice," she pleaded.

I told her a few details about costume fees, practice times, and tryouts, volunteering to give her copies of our past concerts for choreography ideas. She thanked me and said the next time she came to Preston to visit she would stop by to pick up the materials.

When Joanna came to my home bubbling over with excitement, I gave her a big hug, shook hands with her husband, and admired her baby. I tried to give her all the encouragement I could, then spoke to her husband, "Whether or not Joanna is successful depends a lot on your willingness to support her. The help of a good man makes all the difference in such an endeavor."

He nodded, "I intend to be there for her."

"I'm glad to hear it," I said and thought of my own good man.

Several months later Joanna called again to give me the update. "You won't believe what happened," Joanna began. A large majority of the students in this high school are from Mexico, and when I tried to teach them the cha-cha after tryouts, they were angry. They said it was not the kind of dancing they learned in Mexico and wanted to do their own style of dance. I didn't know what to do, because I don't know their dances. I tried to explain to them that I only know the kind of dancing we do here. Only a couple of people showed up at the next practice."

"Alexis, I had to give in and told them, 'Okay, tell your friends to come back, and I will do what they want to do.'"

"Oh, Joanna, I can't believe it. What happened next?"

"Well, I was able to keep them happy by having them show me their steps. Then I tried to organize them, using formations and throwing in some lifts and drops. We are learning to get along, and I think it will be okay now."

"What a challenge you have. You did the right thing by learning their dance," I told her. "Maybe later they will let you show them one of your dances. But think of it. You may be keeping these teenagers from getting into gangs and terrible mischief."

"You know, Alexis, this is really hard. It is stressful and so much work, but for some reason I can't stop. I have a burning desire to keep going."

I smiled thinking that, in spite of all my own hardships in the past, I, too, had a burning desire motivating me. "I know just how you feel, Joanna. I can't stop either. Too much good comes from it. You are developing character and changing lives."

They weren't just words, for I believed it profoundly. Many of my students went on to teach at high schools, some only for awhile. But whenever they did, it had an influence.

It was common for many of my students to become members of Preston High School's Student Exec Council each year. Over a ten-year period, six student body presidents were ballroom dancers. It is probable that performing in front of large audiences gave them confidence to run for student office.

One president named Sawyer loved Latin dancing and was full of enthusiasm for life—a happy, positive soul—no one could help but like him. He dreamed up many fun activities at the high school. His most successful was a rendition of "Dancing with the Stars"—a spin-off of the popular TV show.

He asked six of my most experienced ballroom students to teach dances to six successful high school teens who hadn't danced.

The stars included the top wrestler who won a State Championship, a great football player, the head cheerleader, an award winner in the Future Farmers of America program, a female basketball star, and a top male baseball player. Each learned a different dance choreographed by the instructor.

Sawyer went all out on advertising, making the whole town aware of it. The high school gym was packed. When I showed up that night, I couldn't believe the elaborate decorations with large strips of fabric as backdrops, balloons, glittery stars, and wooden life-size figures of dancers.

It was a melodramatic affair with emcees and vivacious judges playing it up to the hilt. The program was filled in with local talent, as well as the Exec Council members jumping up and down to their own funky dance. The newly-elected, fall officers danced a comical hip hop routine that had us in stitches.

It was a night of sheer entertainment that involved a host of individuals. The contestants did a great job and expressed their appreciation of this new-found love.

I had to chuckle at the football player's response. His partner was the graceful and irresistible Priscilla, dressed in a long, sequined gown that flared below her hips. When asked what he liked about participating, he responded with, "All of it."

What young man wouldn't want to foxtrot around the room with a doll like that?

Taylee King taught a New York Hustle to the championship wrestler, and they were the first place winners for the night.

After the show, I went up to Sawyer to congratulate him on the successful evening and the huge community turnout. With a glowing face he said, "You are my inspiration, Alexis!" and he threw his arms around me.

The following week in the *Preston Citizen* was an article about a dance extravaganza to be held on the high school football field. I attended the event and witnessed twelve hundred elementary school children do dances from many different countries. The mother of one of my students was in charge. I was thrilled to see dance incorporated into the curriculum. *Preston*, I thought, *has become quite the dancing community.*

Winners of "Dancing with the Stars"

Chapter 34

The Poetry of Dance

Dancing fulfilled a real need I had to express emotion. But I also had a need to verbally express emotion, my joy in dancing. Somehow I had to get it out, like a hatchling needing to burst out of its shell. Poetry was the best means. I discovered someone else felt as I did when I opened the local newspaper one morning and found a published, artistic poem written by one of my dance students, Nathan Nartker.

Dancing

The rhythm moves the inner self
Lost in the music divine
One can feel a surge of passion
That envelops and dominates the mind

Gliding across a silver cloud
To feel the gentle swell of the wind
The floor no longer connects
Into flight, it sends

Two figures in movement unite
Pulling away, yet embracing as one
Twist and twirl and find
Joyous fulfillment when done.

Nathan had composed the rhyme for a young poets' competition. It was one of the top ten chosen out of his grade division with thousands of entries, and he won a $50 savings bond.

I could relate to Nathan's desire to express his love of dance. I decided to share my attempt with my class.

"For the message this morning," I began, "I hope you don't mind if I share a poem I wrote. Sometimes I am frustrated because it isn't appropriate to get up and dance whenever I get the urge. Maybe you feel the same way. "

The Bird Within

Lovely music fills the room,
My heart begins to race.
Deep inside the beauty blooms
And finds a special place.

Convention holds me in my chair.
It binds and ties me down.
I wish to leap up in the air
Give flight to what I've found.

It turns to love without a doubt.
I dare not it confine.
Artistic joy I must dance out
Within my dreaming mind.

I swirl and twirl, sway to and fro.
I do a dip or two,
Yet as I sit here nothing shows
The bird within that flew.

The look in their eyes said, "We understand."

When I attended one of BYU's ballroom dance concerts, a particular number had special significance to me, which used the song, "Dance with My Father." Music is just another form of poetry.

The graceful, young people moved to the lyrical rhythm, acting out the message that touched me deeply as I listened to the following words:

Back when I was a child,
Before life removed all the innocence,
My father would lift me high
And dance with my mother and me
And then spin me around till I fell asleep,
Then up the stairs he would carry me,
And I knew for sure I was loved.

If I could get another chance,
Another walk, another dance with him,
I'd play a song that would never, ever end.
How I'd love, love, love to dance with my father again.
(By Richard Marx and Luther Vandross)

Tears streamed down my face as the meaning, music, and motions described the feelings of my heart. What wouldn't I give to have one more dance with my father?

Not long after that I had a dream about Dad. He approached me in a beautiful mountain setting, much like the places we hiked to in the summers when I was young. He began to recite poetry to me. I could not remember the words to the poem when morning dawned, but the message remained. It was something similar to this:

I love my life here in this place.
God has been good to me.
Though we're apart he offers grace
And your sweet days I see.

For me your love has been made known—
A sparkling gem in heart.
My love and prayers for you increase,
Though we are far apart.

Down the road we'll reunite
In this realm heavenly.
The joy compares unto a dance
We share just you and me.

It was so powerful—a dream I could never forget. I pondered on the love I had for my father. Dad must have known of my grand time with ballroom dancing and that I had been writing poetry, something I picked up from him. It gave me so much peace. I was glad he was aware that I was living life to the fullest as he had taught me. The dream filled me with increased hope that I would see my father someday and that I would dance with him again.

The bird that flew - Alexis & David, seniors at BYU

Chapter 35

The Rewards Win Out

It would be a fib to declare that teaching ballroom dancing to young people has few challenges or disappointments. The truth is that it takes a lot of sacrifice, such as, the burden of costuming, collecting fees, and dealing with parents—like the time one father threatened to sue when I kicked his daughter off the team for poor attendance. I had to give her another chance to pacify him. Or there was the mother who came to me bawling that her daughter's life would be ruined if I didn't let her on the team. The stress of trying to get a crowd of teenagers warmed up and on the floor at just the right moment with all their accessories intact was overwhelming. But the good, the great, and the glorious experiences always won out over the difficulties. An example

351

is the following typical experience at the Gem State Competition.

As the bus loaded with fifty excited teenagers, the vehicle echoed with comments like, "Save me a place next to you!" "Did you bring your cards?" "Can I borrow your hairspray later? I forgot mine." "I have Cheetos if anyone wants some."

After the costumes were stored and locked away, I checked my list to make sure everyone had shown up. I knew we were one girl short, since she planned to drive up with her parents.

Suddenly, a man climbed aboard the bus and said, "I was just passing by and saw a clothes bag on the bench over there. Could it belong to anyone here?"

Running to the bench, sure enough, it was a forgotten costume bag. I thanked the stranger, relieved that disaster had been thwarted and gave the bag to the guilty student who approached me apologetically.

I called everyone to order and gave the usual speech. "The reason I am bringing you to this competition at BYU-Idaho campus is so you can see what the other high schools are doing in the world of ballroom dance, hoping it will motivate you. I expect you to do your best. If you make a mistake, pick yourself up and jump right back in again. I won't be angry. To me it is not about winning but doing your best and enjoying the experience."

After a prayer by a volunteer, we were off. The noise from the talkative teens for two and a half hours was always trying to me, especially the older I got. When we arrived, I felt the pressure of getting the large group checked in and settled in dressing rooms.

My fourteen-year-old daughter Karrie had come earlier to compete in a few individual junior competitions, and I visited with her for a few minutes. Then I rounded up my students to rehearse in another building. They ran through our competition numbers, and tension mounted as I tried to correct executions they should already know.

Why are they doing so lousy? I wondered to myself. *Don't they understand they will be performing to thousands of people?* My failure to keep up a standard of professionalism was daunting, the missing girl making it worse.

After a second-rate run through for all three teams, my assistant, Sherri, spoke up. "Okay, we have warmed up and we have lectured you, but from now on we want you to have fun. Do your best and have a great time. Let's meet back at the bus, and we will drive someplace for dinner."

Although Sherri tried to help me keep my perspective, I left the practice room disheartened. Would tonight's performance be a disaster? Why won't they give me more effort? I questioned internally.

Suddenly three former ballroom dance students appeared who were attending the college. The two boys had been part of my birthday surprise. They all hugged me as Joshua announced, "I'm going to the big event tonight! I have to cheer you guys on!"

"Thanks, Joshua." I responded feeling happier. "How is school going?"

"I love it! Dancing on the college team here has been awesome. I am having the best time."

A flash of memories with Joshua passed before my eyes, like the lip-sync he did that could top *American idol*, as the boys held him above their heads and girls danced around him. In a specialty number where he spun a girl holding onto her wrist and ankle, he usually landed her gently on her stomach to end spinning on the floor, but once he accidentally lost his balance causing her to belly flop on the ground. She rolled over to hold her middle. I chuckled inside at the recollection. It was great to see Joshua again.

"Good luck, Alexis," said the other boy.

Standing next to them was Stephanie. She said, "I wouldn't miss it for the world, Alexis. I am excited to see my sister have this chance to perform with you.

I said my goodbyes and met my group on the bus feeling more lighthearted.

We headed to a local area with bountiful fast-food establishments. After giving the students a directive of when to return to the bus before we disembarked, I walked to a restaurant with my daughter, fretting that the students might not return on time. It had happened before.

We sat down to eat, and Karrie bubbled over with excitement about her day of competing. She said she hadn't won anything, but that wasn't important to her. She was happy just to dance. I was glad she had a good perspective. It was nice to see her looking so cheerful and confident.

I shared with her my burden of worrying about supervising such a large group and their disappointing practice. "Don't worry, Mom, she said encouragingly. I'm sure they will give it their best shot at the competition tonight."

Noting my continued apprehension, she suggested we go next door for ice cream. Now that was a happy prospect. I did not know how much until, while ordering, another former student walked in. "What are the chances that

I'd meet you here?" Erica exclaimed as her arms went around me. Pictures came to mind of our five years together, starting with an eighth grade dance class, ending in a beautiful foxtrot solo her senior year with Jason to "Kick in the Head." Besides all that, she was one of Laura's best friends and had been to my home often.

We sat together after we ordered, and I received an update on her life. She was rewarding herself for finishing a very important school exam. She told me she minored in dance, performed with the BYUI team, instructed college dance classes, and taught dance at a nearby high school. We discussed the struggles involved in working with teenagers—coming up with costumes, choreography, and motivating students. I shared my empathy.

"In spite of the challenges," she explained, "I love being creative and seeing students enjoy themselves. It is extremely rewarding. I want to open my own dance studio when I graduate and dance the rest of my life."

I gave her another hug and wished her luck. My steps were light as I walked back to the bus with my daughter. To my surprise no one was late.

At the performing hall I sent my teens to get into their outfits and fix their hair and makeup, admonishing them to return promptly. The competition began and rhythmic music swayed the costumed couples, pulling them this way and that. To me, the next best thing to dancing was watching it. The clever moves thrilled me over and over.

While I waited, I looked around to count how many Preston students had returned from the dressing rooms—very few. They were missing these awesome numbers, and I could not bear it. I ran downstairs to round them up. Some responded and followed me, but the rest dawdled. I hoped they would come soon, but we still had time before our turn. Meanwhile, I sat down to enjoy the show.

There was a beautiful Viennese waltz with long flowing gowns, and a tantalizing cha-cha that made me wiggle in my seat. Just then Leanne sat down next to me. She had driven up from Preston.

"This is so hard!" she blurted out. "I want so desperately to be out there that it hurts to watch. I miss dancing so much!" she moaned.

I remembered how she had put her whole heart into a lift routine she had performed a year ago as a senior. She was working now. We delighted in watching a few more numbers together before she ran off to greet other friends.

The thought came to me that we could ask Leanne to help supervise and teach the B team next year. That way she could still have dancing in her life.

Looking around I noticed many Preston students still missing. With the stress returning, I spoke to those present like a sergeant, "Each of you go find your partner and tell them to get out here right now so we can discuss entrances and exits."

Back sitting by my daughter I agonized, "Where is everybody?"

"Relax, Mom. They will come. Don't worry." I was beginning to get angry. Just then my son's old dance partner, Caroline, sat down by me and threw her arms around my neck. She was attending the college. It never failed. Whenever I felt the load of my responsibility, I was reminded of the rewards and could not be overwhelmed for long.

My daughter and I watched another enticing number—this time a west coast swing. The blues feeling did totally different things to my insides. I had not choreographed one for awhile, and I thought of a west coast dance I would like to teach next year.

Crunch time had come. I rounded up my Standard group to discuss where to enter and exit, relieved the missing girl had arrived in costume.

Still worrying if everyone had listened to my instructions, we approached the floor. I wished them luck and walked over to stand by the music technician. Crossing my fingers, I prayed that everyone did the lifts right. My son Brad, who was among them, gave me a smile.

The team went out on the floor with the announcement, "Preston High School will perform a country dance, choreographed by Sherri Rallison" A fiddle sounded in a toe-tapping rhythm, while the dancers did polka turns, went under bridges and into a grand right and left with spins. At one point, four men each squatted on one leg as they circled their other leg and jumped over it with their hands and spare foot. Then they leaped up, did a spring handstand and slid across the floor on the seat of their pants. Four couples each joined for a king's cross lift—two lines made an X while the men ran in a circle, the girls' legs flying outward as they hung on the side of their partners. The audience clapped to the rhythm.

Next, the girls did a section by themselves. Then the men joined them soon after, and they paired off in four groups. Two girls sat on the arms of two boys as they all faced in a circle. The girls stretched backward, parallel to the ground, and became spinning teeter-totters moving up and down. The dancers did more polka steps and ended with the girls leaping into different poses into the arms of the men at the abrupt ending beat. The atmosphere was thick with a barrage of cheers as they left the floor jumping for joy.

When the awards were distributed, we won second place in our division. Clearly my worries had been in vain. We arrived home that night at one o'clock in the morning, and it took me days to recuperate.

Well, that is what directing a team is like—highs and lows. It involves stress and worry, but it always ends with happy spectators and ecstatic teenagers. It was for that reason that I kept going year after year. The rewards won out, especially when I got a note from a student like Alysha that said, "Being a part of the dance team was one of the funnest things I've ever done!"

Alysha later danced in a college group, became an instructor, minored in dance, and taught a high school team.

Recently, I heard that one of my early soloists, Kevin, named his daughter, "Alexis." Maybe she will turn out to be a dancer.

Polka teeter-totter

Chapter 36

Help in Hard Times

Managing my ballroom program was a challenge but overall, it did wonders for me personally. Working with young people not only gave me a deep sense of fulfillment, but also carried me through some adverse moments, like when my widowed mother was diagnosed with colon cancer.

My siblings and I had six months to get used to the idea of her leaving us. We went into mourning even before she died. She told us not to feel sorry for her, because she was excited to be with my father again. But I felt sorry for myself at the prospect of not seeing her or not being able to call her when I wanted. She was a gifted homemaker and guiding light in my life. I owed her so much and would miss her dreadfully.

Attending ballroom practices was the primary factor in lifting my spirits as my mother's health faded and also after she was gone, for how could I walk into that room with dozens of laughing teenagers moving so cheerfully to vibrant music and not have it pull me out of the pit of sadness? Ballroom was like a special comforter with loving arms; it was there for me through a difficult period of mourning.

This was not only true for myself, but for many others. One of my students named Sam had a suicide in his family. The team members were heartbroken for their friend. Sam was gone for a week while his family mourned and attended the funeral. We mourned with him. His ballroom friends hugged him when he returned to rehearsal. He was touched by their concern. The uplifting environment in class buoyed him up.

As if that had not been enough for that family to bear, Sam was diagnosed with rheumatoid arthritis, a painful disease in young people. His mother called me to explain her son's challenges. "Alexis, if you notice that he doesn't seem to be dancing as well as usual, I just want you to know that he is in a lot of discomfort. Can you please be patient with him? Your husband says that dancing will help keep his muscles toned."

"I have never noticed any change in Sam," I told his mother. "He dances with the same enthusiasm as always. He is not only a great dancer but a wonderful person, and I love having him on the team. I am so sorry about this problem he is facing and hope dancing can keep his mind off his troubles."

"It already has," she responded.

A particular morning after everyone had left ballroom practice, Sherri brought up a concern over a student named Phil. Phil's mother had confided to Sherri that Phil suffered from depression. The mother asked Sherri to keep an eye on him and call her if he ever seemed to have real despair. Worried by teen suicide on the news, she was trying to be realistic that it could happen in her own family.

Sharing my observations, I said, "Phil does look down at times, Sherri, but only when he first comes to class. He never leaves practice looking sad. In fact, he always charges out the door higher than a kite. Tell his mother that she doesn't need to worry about him while he is here. Dancing seems to lift him up." Sherri agreed with me.

The situation proved to me that dancing could be very useful in combating depression, helping to produce endorphins.

The storms of life often discouraged my young friends, but dancing provided a harbor. Through the small-town grapevine, I heard that several of my students had difficult home lives. Class time provided a positive environment in contrast, offering a place of acceptance. Conquering dance steps built self-esteem in troubled students, while friendships became an anchor, giving them strength to endure their rough circumstances.

I found similar strength from ballroom. When my adult children began to have hardships, it was easy for me to stew and worry about them. Choreography, planning, and teaching came to my rescue by keeping my mind off their struggles.

One night, however, I was so overwhelmed with gloom and concern for one child in particular I didn't know how to overcome it. Kneeling by my bed, I prayed for the Lord to comfort me, then climbed under the covers and slowly drifted off.

I dreamed that I was at home pacing the floor fretfully, when all of a sudden the door opened and past ballroom students walked in filling my living room. Many I hadn't seen for years, but they were still as dear to me as my own family. One by one, with their eyes overflowing with the tears and precious memories, they put their arms around me. I shared my unique feelings for each of them, finally asking, "Why are you here?"

One spoke for them all, "We just wanted to be with you tonight. We want you to know how much you mean to us and that we love you."

My heartache dissolved and I awoke to a room enveloped with love, giving me peace.

One of my student's favorite quotes was printed in the school yearbook. It described the situation perfectly, "God gave us memories so that we may have roses in the December of our lives." (Sir James M. Barry) Happy times with ballroom friends saw me through some tough December days. Little did I know that the dream prophesied of a day to come.

Bonded ballroom dancers

Tragedy struck our family when Laura's husband, Adam, was diagnosed with an aggressive Lymphoma cancer only a year and a half after they were married. By then they had a little baby girl. He had to quit college to undergo chemotherapy, and was deathly ill from the effects. During this time, Laura and Adam's ballroom friends did what they could. Giovanni took Adam hunting and fishing when possible. Laura's girlfriends visited and emailed. It was a difficult time for them, but eventually Adam went into remission.

Laura told me about their special date to a Valentine's dance. "Oh, Mom, after that horrible year Adam went through, do you know what it was like for me to dance with him again? Now that he was finally feeling better, we danced the whole time and didn't rest. We were amazed that we could still remember all we had learned. It was euphoric, Mom. It was a night I will never forget."

They had great hopes that Adam's cancer would be cured, but whatever the outcome, he and Laura wanted another child—a companion for their firstborn. Laura became pregnant again. Unfortunately, a few days before the baby was due, Adam's fever returned, the signal that all was not well. Scans showed his cancer had returned with a vengeance.

The week of Thanksgiving Adam returned to the hospital for radiation. Luckily, the tumor near his heart responded by shrinking, allowing him to leave shortly to be with Laura, who was about to give birth. Laura, Adam and I spent Thanksgiving Day in the hospital with their new baby girl, born the night before.

The sweet picture will be forever etched in my mind of Laura and Adam lying side by side in the hospital bed gloating over the precious bundle, with a look of pride and love. Even in those dark circumstances, a ray of light came through the clouds to light up the world for just a moment making us thankful.

The moment didn't last long. Adam was in and out of the hospital with more treatments. Ballroom friends of high school days kept in contact with words of encouragement. But the cancer was aggressive and did its work. Through the sessions ahead, Adam was gentle, kind, and uncomplaining, carrying the burden like a stalwart soldier trying to keep a determined face for home and family. We were so proud of him.

As February commenced, the reality that he would not be coming home from the hospital hit like a grenade, shattering our dreams. As his pain intensified, the visits and help from friends came daily.

Close to the end, Adam went into a coma. God knew in Laura's heart and that she wanted to say one last goodbye. While she was lying next to him in his hospital bed, he opened his eyes and looked at her. She said, "I love you, Adam. We'll be together forever, right?"

He nodded, smiled, and put his arms around her for the last time, falling unconscious again.

A few hours later the battle was lost, but with it came relief for an end to his suffering. Laura was grateful for her last goodbye. We sadly resigned ourselves to God's will, finding no answer as to why such things happen, continuing in faith and hope in the Lord's resurrection.

Laura came home to flowers and condolence calls. The dream I had had years before, where my students offered comfort, came to pass. Seven ballroom friends appeared at our home a few nights later to offer their sympathy. Wrapped in hugs and tears, we relived the past, laughing at the silly and fabulous times together, recounting Adam's virtues that left us in awe.

At the Sunday evening viewing over thirty ballroom friends who knew Adam came to pay their respects along with four hundred others.

When Jason approached us bawling his eyes out, I said, "It's a real kick in the head, isn't it, Jason?"

He laughed through his tears and said, "It sure is."

My dancing birthday boys all came and recounted the fun of popping out of boxes with Adam to dance for me. Michelle, my first soloist was there, as well as Annie who played a bride in my first medley. Rachael and Rusty, who had married, offered condolences. Rachael was expecting her third child. Mac who loved dance came with his dancing sisters, as well as Launie, who had learned a lesson in friendship. Most of the kids from the eighth grade class I taught showed up. Mr. and Mrs. King put their arms around us, told us how they loved Adam, and extolled the good that dancing had been for their children. I saw Serina who had done a solo with Rich King, and Jamie, my Mary in the dancing nativity. The Crosland family offered their sympathy and I treasured the chance to hold each one—Malia, Giovanni, Arianna, Armando, Mario, and Marco—like pearls of great price. They had grown up with Adam and felt the loss. Sherri and her children were present as well. It was a gigantic reunion of family, loved ones, lifetime associates, and ballroom buddies pouring out love that cushioned the blow, giving us strength to go on.

After the beautiful funeral, Adam was laid to rest in his beloved Mink Creek, on a hill overlooking the canyon area where he loved to hunt and fish. Laura's pals never forgot her and stayed in contact, ever supportive.

Laura and her daughters moved back home with David and me. Two weeks after Adam's death, Laura made a trip to kissing rock on the anniversary of their first kiss. Although Laura tried her best to cope, I knew she needed the medicine that had come to my rescue during hard times—ballroom dancing.

The next year Laura taught the Preston High team a country two-step—a dance she and Adam had learned together in a class at BYU. She also taught a beautiful four-couple, lift routine to a song from a Superman movie where Lois Lane sings to her man of steel. Besides giving Laura incentive to get up every day, ballroom class helped her make new friends. Dancing stirred happy chemicals within her being, rejuvenating her. Ballroom friendships had supported her through the worst, and dancing again gave her something to look forward to.

At the warm-up practice before her students were to perform the lift number for the first time, she gathered them around to share her feelings. "I want you to know that this dance means a lot to me. It hasn't been easy for me to do this. Ten months ago today my husband passed away. I love that we're doing this song because for me, dancing with Adam was always like dancing with superman. He lifted me with such ease and twirled me around the dance floor so gracefully it felt like flying. When you go out there tonight, you are Superman and Lois Lane, but to me you also represent my own great love story and I consider each performance, a performance for Adam."

The students took her words to heart and danced the number beautifully, helping Laura express her emotions and pay tribute.

For our finale number I choreographed a country swing, my tribute to Adam. He was an avid fisherman, so I chose the song "Fishin' in the Dark." As I pondered on the necessary formations, I came up with the idea to have the dancers form individual letters in a message— the message "I love you." At the ending of the song, I had all the students drop on the ground to make a picture with their bodies— the picture of a fish. My friends enjoyed sharing the message of my heart through ballroom dance, a tribute to my oustanding son who loved to dance.

I received a couple of plaques from friends that expressed what I was learning in reality. One had the words, "Life may not always be the party we hoped for, but while we are here we might as well dance." Another said, "Life isn't about waiting for the storm to pass. It's about learning to dance in the rain."

Laura and Adam Beardall

Chapter 37

Gratitude

Two weddings happened to take place on the same beautiful August day in Preston. They involved former ballroom students of mine. Many of the people attending both garden receptions were dancing friends. Every time I turned around I was being hugged. We reveled in memories and being together once again.

Paige's mother approached me and said, "Paige was thrilled you were able to go down to Provo to see her perform with the BYU team. She loves you so much."

I responded by saying, "You know Mrs. Christensen, last week I visited Sue Jensen, the woman who taught me to dance. I love and appreciate her so deeply. I have only been trying to pass on what she did for me. One day someone will love Paige profoundly because of what she does for them." Mrs. Christensen said she understood.

I was part of a chain that I hoped would continue.

Although I tried to keep Sue updated about our dancing successes, I kept feeling that she did not quite understand the breadth and depth of her influence or how far it had gone. One day when we talked on the phone, I began to cry as I tried to express my appreciation and told her my dream was to have her come to a Preston concert where I could present her to my community and give her the credit she deserved. She said she would be there in April.

The night of the concert, I handed out programs at the door, waiting impatiently for Sue and her husband Reid to make an entrance. Reid had always been very supportive of his wife and was a great guy who I loved dearly. They arrived as promised, and to my surprise Sue and I were both wearing the color red, perfect symbolism of all the sacrifices we had made over the years to teach young people, but also representing the love in our hearts.

Putting my arms around them, I thanked them for coming. They took their seats. When it was time to start, I spoke into the microphone,

"Ladies and Gentlemen, I want to welcome you to our Preston High School Ballroom Dance Concert. We wish to thank our superintendent, school administrators, the athletic director, teachers, and our school secretaries for all their support and help with our program. We appreciate the parents for getting students to rehearsals and performances."

I called Sue down out of the audience. "Tonight I would like to present to you someone who is very special to me. Her name is Susan Jensen. She is the woman who first taught me how to dance." There were exclamations in the audience. I told the story of my first ballet class and all the dance festivals that followed, which led to my dancing in college, meeting my husband, and becoming a dance teacher.

"I want to thank Sue publicly for all she has done for me." The audience applauded. I handed her a gift and put my arm around her. She was embarrassed with the attention, but it was something I had to do.

My teams performed with the usual gusto filling us with happiness. After the concert, the Jensens came down to visit with me. Sue began with, "Oh, Alexis, you are doing such wonderful things in this town. They danced so well. It was a fabulous concert, and I am so glad we came."

Reid reiterated the same feelings. I introduced them to my family and friends. The night was the highlight of the year for me.

Sue opened the present and loved the ballerina figurine I gave her. I told her to remember me every time she looked at it. She said she would.

After everyone went their own way, my husband took me in his arms to move as one around the dance floor in an International Style foxtrot.

"You still haven't lost your touch, Big Boy!" I whispered in his ear.

He smiled. "You know, I just may come out of retirement."

"What?" I responded. "It's been at least ten years since you've done a solo with me. You mean you would consider performing next year?"

"Why, not?" he said. "I'm still as smooth as ever."

With my lips against his ear, I whispered, "Yeah, smooth."

David made good on his promise a year later, and we enjoyed rehearsing for a solo once more, even though we felt pretty rusty now in our fifties. I noticed that the extra time together was good for our relationship and made us appreciate one another even more.

When the word got out that we were performing at the concert, people expressed their excitement at seeing us take the floor again. One of David's patients said, "This is something I'd kill to see."

Before our number, I told the audience that David's grandmother had given him his tuxedo when he was twenty-one and amazingly he could still wear it. The audience laughed and clapped.

I walked out holding David's hand in a lavish ballroom gown made by my friend, Becky. The music started, and off we went in an International foxtrot to Frank Sinatra's "Yes, Sir, That's My Baby." Dad and I both loved Frank Sinatra. My students grinned at us from the back corner. It had been a long time since we had performed, but it was still just as much fun. Partway through, he took me into a throwaway oversway where we lunged and opened up to pose. I arched my head back as far as I could to smile at the audience. Chuckles broke out. Floating through space was a touch of heaven. At the end, David took me into a dip and planted a big juicy kiss on my lips. The audience roared.

A friend commented to me afterward, "The kiss was my favorite part."

"It was my favorite part, too," I said.

At the end of the program, the thirteen graduating seniors presented me with a beautiful picture of themselves all dressed in different colored costumes with the words, "Thanks for Adding Color to our Lives." I couldn't help but think that is what they had done for me.

In the year 2010, Brigham Young University celebrated the fiftieth anniversary of the ballroom dance program. Special effort was made to contact all alumni and invite them to this multiple-day event. David had other obligations, so I went down Friday by myself. He would come the following day. When the alumni met at the campus ballroom for a huge, general meeting, surprisingly among the hundreds of people present, the first person I ran into was Neal Swann. I hadn't seen him since the first year I started my program. I put my arm around him and thanked him for teaching my husband how to dance. He responded with, "Oh, I had a lot of fun teaching that class."

Moving on, I watched for other acquaintances. Happiness ricocheted off the walls hitting everyone as old friends found one another and chatted excitedly. The emcee delayed starting the meeting because of the blissful reuniting. Then

I saw Randy and his wife. Randy had been the President of the International teams when I was at BYU. We had kept in touch through Christmas cards for the past thirty years, but I hadn't seen him since school. We got caught up on the basics of our lives. He had children attending Brigham Young University now.

"Randy, you were our inspiration. You always beat everyone in the competitions and our goal was to try to beat you. But you were never surpassed. You were incredible."

He laughed. "Oh, I think you are exaggerating, but thanks for the compliment."

Randy was a first-class guy and an inspiring leader. He had gone on to marry his dance partner and raise a fine family.

Next, I saw Becky and we hugged. She had done the early sewing for my team. I had missed her when she had moved to Kansas. "It is so good to see you," I said.

She told me about other team members she recognized, and we sat down for the meeting that started.

The BYU director was the emcee and he led us through a costume show where current tour team members modeled past ballroom attire. They came out with a short series of dance maneuvers hamming it up. We cheered for the costumes we had once danced in and went into hysterics over the funny, one-piece cat suits they used to wear in the 80's.

During the program, videos were played describing ballroom history at BYU, and Blackpool performances. High on memories, the glory days, the friendships, and every golden moment, it all came back, overwhelmingly. Everyone felt the euphoria of it. I'd never seen a room of more ecstatic people.

When past directors were introduced, a chill ran through me as Emerson Lyman stood. I was happy to see he was still living. I had not been able to keep in contact with him and looked forward to seeing him later. He hadn't changed and was as handsome as ever with his white hair. I owed the man so much. The training I received from him had blessed so many.

A high point of the meeting took place when the audience demanded past directors, Lee and Linda Wakefield, to demonstrate the T-press. They took over BYU's dance program after Mr. Lyman left. Lee & Linda had won two United States National Professional Theater Arts Championships with their adagio numbers. Lee had to be at least sixty years old now, but he whipped up thin Linda into position and held her over his head like a young man. The crowd went crazy with screams, laughter, and clapping. The audience stood. Lee kept holding her up there grinning with satisfaction as the crowd continued their approval. I couldn't believe how long he sustained the pose. What a man! Lee was one of a kind. He and his wife led the BYU Ballroom Dance Company to seventeen British Formation titles. His students established high school teams all over the Wasatch Front.

I appreciated Lee's help when I started my team. He gave me a video of syllabus steps, and I attended his classes at the BYU Adult Ballroom dance camps. I remembered the fun of demonstrating the tango with him in one class, when there weren't enough men to go around.

Afterward we dispersed and met in different rooms according to the years we were with the company. There I rejoiced at seeing my old friends from the Latin, Standard, and Social teams. I marveled at how successful they had all become. Many told me of the difficult challenges they had struggled with since college. Life was not easy. But we were bound by our love for each other, dance, and the beautiful memories we shared.

I made my way across the room to Mr. Lyman. I put my arm around him, kissed his cheek, and said, "Remember me?"

He was quiet, searching his memory. I reminded him of a few events, which brought back his recollection. Then I told him about my fifteen years of instructing Preston's high school team and the astounding consequences. His face lit up. He gave me a squeeze and said he was happy I had continued to dance and share it with others. He wrote down his address for me so I could continue to inform him of my group. Before I left him, I said, "I owe you so much. Thank you for everything you have done for me." He looked pleased that he had been of value to someone else—that maybe his life had deep significance.

What goes around comes around. The next day my family and I attended the matinee of the BYU Ballroom Dance Company Concert. It started out with an alumni dance. What fun! I hadn't had time to come down earlier to learn the routine and be involved, but I loved picking out old friends among the group. The mass of alumni filled up the huge floor at the Marriot Center three times, with one set of dancers running off as another came on. They were having a stupendous time, still maintaining their sparkle in the limelight. A true performer has a certain presentation, and they still had it, despite the years that had passed.

As I continued to watch the program, the current college team demonstrated a peak of mastery in their dancing. Holding the audience in the palm of their hands from beginning to end, the time flew by. I recognized two participants as former Preston High team members—Tim and Paige. Tim danced a quickstep solo for me years before and Paige had been a waltz soloist. They looked elegant and happy.

After the concert, people swarmed toward the exits. I lost track of Paige, but I could see Tim on the stage floor. Tim's family had moved from Preston after he graduated from high school, so I hadn't seen him for years. I fought my way through the crowd, anxious to reach Tim.

A female usher blocked the entryway to the main floor. I asked her if I could pass.

"No one is allowed down there," she said firmly. I backed away disappointed. Then I tried yelling Tim's name to attract his attention, but he couldn't hear me.

I went back over to the usher and tried again. "You don't understand. I taught that boy how to dance. I know he would want to see me. Please let me through."

"You are going to get me fired," she said, and graciously let me pass. I ran down the stairs and across the stage.

"Tim!" I yelled. He turned and recognized me.

"Alexis!" He wrapped me up in a hug that lifted me off the floor. "I am so glad you were able to come!" Tim beamed. "I can't begin to tell you how much I love dancing. Do you have any idea how much I think of you? I owe it all to you — all this joy and happiness."

I knew that joining the BYU Dance Company now took a lot more training than when I was young, the competition being steep. Tim had taken many classes and practiced intensely to get where he was. He didn't stop for me to speak, so I smiled.

"Oh, Alexis, I just tried out for the backup touring team for the fall and I made it. I can't get over it. My dance partner and I have worked so hard. We did really well at the last competition and won out many of the tour team members. Can you believe it?! My partner is so wonderful. She and I have the same burning desire to dance."

"Tim, I am glad you are enjoying yourself. Do I detect a romantic interest in this partner?"

"Yes." He cracked a sideways smile.

"You see, in the past she had a couple of guys get serious too soon, and she is really nervous about getting into a relationship."

Mentally, I said, *Uh huh, gun-shy.* I remembered the feeling well.

"So, I am trying to keep it cool, just be friends, and concentrate on dance right now. Maybe it will turn into something more later on. I am hoping it will."

He continued, "She is so wonderful!"

I laughed. "It sounds like history repeating itself."

Tim went on and on about what dancing meant to him. Then he suggested, "Hey, how about if I perform a solo at your next concert?"

"Oh, Tim, I would love that. Let's plan on it."

He hugged me again, said goodbye, and disappeared into the dark. I found myself alone on the huge floor of the darkened Marriot Center flooded in what felt like purple moonlight. I looked up at the curtain that had a projected picture of an elegantly-costumed couple in a curtsey and bow with the words *Encore* above them. I stared at it for a long time seeing my life before my eyes.

How different everything would have been without dance. What if Sue had never taught that skinny, thirteen-year-old girl? What if I never tried out for the BYU dance team? What if I had never started a high school program? There were the countless thrilling performances, and important principles learned. There were young people who had stayed on track because of positive associations, dancing romances that had turned to weddings, and of course lifetimes filled with fun, all the result of dance. I felt intense gratitude to those who had given so much of their lives to teach me and thankful for the friends I had made.

I have never regretted listening to my father's advice to "dance to live!" And I never will.

Alexis and David, foxtrot solo

Tim Colvin

Epilogue

Tim Colvin came to Preston with his partner like he planned, also bringing a BYU Latin couple with him. I opened the gym early for them to practice. As I watched, I couldn't believe the height of perfection Tim had reached in his dancing. It far surpassed what I had done in college. He had won many competitions. While Tim and his friends rested, I shared with him something that was special to me.

"One night a few years ago I had a dream where I danced with a world-class ballroom dancer. We did an International-Style foxtrot that was exquisitely wonderful. I never felt anything so beautiful in my whole life. When I woke up, I said to myself, 'Well, that is what heaven is like. It can't get any better than that.'"

Tim replied, "Oh, but it *is* so much better than that."

At the concert Tim and his partner performed a gorgeous American waltz and foxtrot, their flow and grace breathtaking. His friends' exacting Latin numbers were also riveting. The BYU students were the highlight of the show.

After the program Tim invited me to dance a foxtrot with him and led me through it expertly. It was pure paradise. When the song ended, another foxtrot tune began. Tim invited me to continue. I said yes! It was a little more complicated, but all the more thrilling. We were angels with wings.

When it concluded, I thanked Tim and walked over to his sister, Erica who exclaimed, "Oh, Alexis, watching the two of you dance that beautifully made me cry."

I wanted to cry, too, but I was too happy. Tim didn't know it, but he made my dream come true that night. He gave me a taste of heaven. The joy I felt at seeing him reach such a state of perfection in that stunning art form was beyond anything.

Erica Colvin started a dance studio in Logan, Utah after she graduated from college. She held weekly dances and gave lessons and workshops to my team members. For engaged couples who wanted to dance at their wedding, Erica taught them steps to make their special day all the more precious. She also wrote articles for the USA Dance magazine. More people are dancing in the Logan, Utah area because of her.

Paige Christensen came back to Preston after she graduated from BYU and taught dancing and technique for Preston High. All my students loved her.

Stephanie Olsen choreographed a rumba solo for her sister, Jaclyn, and also a Viennese solo for her youngest sister, Madilyn, when they were on the Preston Standard team. Each performed at our spring concert. Stephanie's goal is to start her own high school team in Wyoming someday.

Autumn Coats' West Side High School team did joint performances with Preston High School's team for many years. Autumn's group joined with their school band to put on an annual dinner dance called "Moonlight Serenade" with over four hundred people attending.

Ian Porter danced with the BYU-Idaho team and taught with the Arthur Murray studio in Southern California in the summers. He came back to Preston, helped me teach the Preston High team, and choreographed a solo that he performed with his sister, Lena.

Neal Swann's youngest daughter, Jodee, danced for my group for several years also.

Dixon Bowles, my Latin dancer who did the quickstep duet with Brad, performed a gorgeous Viennese Waltz solo his senior year with Stephanie's sister, Madilyn. He put on a dancing production for his senior project, obtained a dance scholarship to Weber State University, and wants to teach in a dance studio someday.

Priscilla Hobbs made the BYU, Provo Ballroom Dance Company as a freshman, which wasn't surprising at all.

"Dancing with the Stars" was repeated at the high school. My daughter Karrie participated, teaching a waltz to a school celebrity. She was voted "Most Elegant."

Eleven years after he graduated, I received an email from Gary Hansen:

Dear Alexis,
Little did I know how the decision to tryout for your team would affect the rest of my life. I have been an active dancer ever since. I've been on college teams and have taught other people the joy of dancing. It's all thanks to you. I wouldn't be the person I am today without all the work, blood, and time you put into teaching us young folks how to dance. I just wanted to email you a little note that you affected my life in such a positive way that I can never repay and give you enough thanks for giving me that opportunity so many years ago. You really did change my life for the better.

After graduating from high school, six Preston students danced on the Utah State team, fourteen danced with the Brigham Young University-Idaho team, seven danced with the Brigham Young University team in Provo, and one danced at Dixie College. Eight taught for high school teams.

A large portion of Preston students were involved in dance in some way after high school, either taking classes, teaching young people in their communities, or dancing socially for their own delight.

Six Preston ballroom couples married when the boys came back from missions for their church. More romances are in the works.

I have been teaching dancing at the Preston High School for sixteen years and am still going strong.

Proceeds from this book will be used to promote ballroom dancing at Preston High and in the Preston community.

Acknowledgments

I wish to thank my sister, Ruth Champneys Cooper, for her ideas on how to present this work and her time in editing it. As a talented English major and author, she was of invaluable service and I appreciate her encouragement. I could not have done this without her.

Kristy Olsen, my sister-in-law and a former magazine editor, was also helpful in editing this book. My editor at Ecko House Publishing, Andy Carter, made some terrific suggestions. I am grateful for the input of these women and the publishing staff of Ecko House that made *Dance to Live* come together.

Dance With My Father
Words by Luther Vandross and Richard Marx
Music by Luther Vandross
© 2003 EMI APRIL MUSIC INC., UNCLE
RONNIE'S MUSIC CO. and CHRYSALIS MUSIC
All Rights for UNCLE RONNIE'S MUSIC CO.
Controlled and Administered by EMI APRIL MUSIC
INC. All Rights for CHRYSALIS MUSIC Controlled
and Administered by BMG CHRYSALIS All Rights
Reserved International Copyright Secured Used by
Permission
Reprinted by Permission of Hal Leonard Corporation